THE WAY OF THE GODDESS

Today the revival of interest in occult beliefs and practices is firmly centred in the return to the Goddess — the veneration of the Universal Feminine Principle which has for so long been neglected in our society.

This book — a practical manual for self-initiation — shows how each of us can follow the Way of the Goddess, rediscovering the wisdom of Earth and Moon with a vision that is both intimate and profound.

Ly Warren-Clarke, herself a practising Wiccan priestess, provides a practical overview of all the key rituals featuring the Goddess through the cycle of the seasons, including rituals for the Equinoxes and Solstices, and a complete guide to the traditional rituals of Samhain, the Bride, Beltaen and Oimelc.

The Way of the Goddess is destined to become a classic in occult literature and a worthy companion to such books as Starhawk's *The Spiral Dance* and Janet & Stewart Farrar's *The Witches' Way*.

"This book summons beautifully the evocative, mythic processes which are at the very heart of witchcraft. *The Way of the Goddess* is a masterwork in the tradition of practical magic."

— Nevill Drury
Author of *The Occult Experience*
and *Vision Quest*

THE WAY
OF THE GODDESS

A Manual for
Wiccan Initiation

Ly Warren-Clarke

PRISM · UNITY

The author acknowledges the use of copyright material from *An ABC of Witchcraft Past and Present* and *Witchcraft for Tomorrow* by Doreen Valiente including *inter alia The Charge of the Goddess*, the Midsummer and Autumn Equinox rituals, Invocation of the Horned God and Invocation to the Goddess of the Moon (pp. 85/6, 95, 98/9, 102-108, 113, 117, 119, 121/3 and 129/30).

Published in Great Britain, 1987 by
PRISM PRESS
2 South Street, Bridport,
Dorset DT6 3NQ

and

Distributed in the USA by
Avery Publishing Group,
350 Thorens Avenue,
Garden City Park,
N.Y. 11040

Published in Australia, 1987 by
UNITY PRESS
Lindfield
N.S.W. 2070

ISBN 1 85327 006 7

Cover illustration: Linda Garland

Typeset in Baskerville by Maggie Spooner Typesetting, London
Printed by The Guernsey Press Ltd., The Channel Islands.

CONTENTS

Prologue   1

Introduction   5

Part One: The Disciplines   11

Section One — First Stage Technique Requirements   13
The Centre   13
Meditation   14
Visualisation   17
Self-analysis Techniques   22
The Flow Affirmation   26

Section Two — Second Stage Technique Progressive   29
Realms of Accessibility   29
Astral Projection   38
Chant and Power Breathing   42
The Mirror   44
Colour   45
Number Symbolism   47
Planetary Symbolism   50
Tarot   54

Part Two: Way of the Goddess   61

The Beginning   62
The Goddess and the God of the Witch   63
The Moon and the Sun   65
The Four Elements   67
The Working Tools of a Witch   72

The Ritual of New Moon   80
The Ritual of Esbat (Full Moon)   83
The Ritual of the Dark Moon   88
The Sabbats: 92
— The Ritual of the Winter Solstice   94
— The Ritual of the Spring Equinox   97
— The Ritual of the Summer Solstice   101
— The Ritual of the Autumn Equinox   105
— The Ritual of Samhain   109
— The Feast of the Bride   112
— The Ritual of Beltaen   116
— The Ritual of Oimelc   119
A Self-Initiation   124
Some Examples of a 'Working'   131
The House Blessing   132
The Practising Witch   133

Table of Correspondences:
— The Elements   136
— Planetary Symbols   137
Suggested Reading   139

Prologue

Within the corner of a darkened room a woman sits upon a chair and hums a repetitive tune. Her eyes are closed and she rocks back and forth, back and forth, back and forth — seeming to sway in some invisible wind like the rushes on a lake shore. Her hands are moving between threads as she weaves and plaits them, every now and then stopping to tie a knot; the silence more permeable for the lack of song.

She sits, thus, for hours until the room lightens with the glow of the rising moon, the shafts of which pierce the window to land at her feet.

The monotonous humming stops, the rocking stops, the dancing fingers stop, her eyes are open.

She stands and walks to the centre of the little room where her table is set with the instruments of her birthright — **Cup**, picking up the glow of moonlight and dripping it onto the cloth beneath; **Knife** with the hilt as black as jet that glints with streaks of silver that have been set into the ancient runes that surround the base and with blade that flares and tapers finely to its point of power; **Pentacle** that glows with burnished light, the symbols upon its face deep and meaningless to any save its owner; **Wand** of Willow wood, finely carven with her own hand into an intricate set of swirls and relief, worn in places where it has been worked lovingly; unlit **Candles** of purest white to compliment the moon's glow and a heavy silver medallion, older than even she knows, that has been passed down, along with the knowledge, from one to the other, in secret nights and ancient tongue, until to her it was bequeathed and all that belongs to the Passage; a **Bowl** of burning coals which glows and sheds its warmth around itself, upon which she drops juniper twigs and wood from the dead bough of an apple tree. From the coals she lights a taper, then the candles, one by one — all in silence and certainty of what is to follow.

Her shapeless dress is unbuttoned and dropped to the floor; her hair, bound about her head in a tight braid, is unravelled and spreads around her in a burnished copper haze. The medallion she takes lovingly within her hands and greets with a soft kiss before raising it to the Moon's glow for approval; she then drops it over her head onto her breast drawing comfort from its familiar coldness upon her skin.

She kneels, raises her arms above her head, breathes deeply and waits. Very soon the Moon is fully risen and the shafts of silver cover her body and radiate around her. She cries out, in the ancient tongue of the Lands of Lirien, that she is ready to greet the Goddess, whose name rings around her thrice, like the chiming of bells.

And the air is still and expectant.

She slowly stands and takes the Cup, its crystal contents brimming over the edge, and walks around the little room sprinkling as she goes. A soft, melodious chant is rising from her as she quickens her pace leaving trails of moonlight glowing in a circle all around her. She feels the force-field, an almost imperceptible swishing that grows to a hum. When it is constant she stops, moves back to her table, proclaiming it to be the Altar. Now she dips the Wand into the Cup and uses the sacred water to seal her body from all things impure or mundane. She kisses its tip and lays it back upon the Altar. She refuels the Brazier and breathes the sweet-smelling smoke — a tribute to her Goddess. She takes the Pentacle between two hands and raises it above her head, calling forth the force of the Four Winds to act as Sentinels to her Rite. She takes the Knife, the Power of her birth-right, and presses it to her breast to fill it with her own essence and then she kneels. The Knife is now Athame. She raises it slowly; her whole being is poured from its tip in shafts of blue fire as she pierces the night for the acknowledgement she knows will come.

Her breath is still. The night is still. The forces of Life wait expectantly and suddenly the light returns to flood the room and the Priestess of the Moon cries out to the Primordial Mother, to whom she was bequeathed before the Dawn of Time. The Mother answers with the heartbreak of a thousand, million lives and acknowledges the Child. They fuse and are one, the cycle is complete, and the Priestess of the Moon is assured; the Magic of her fingers will soothe where they lay, the Magic of her voice will heal where it is heard, the Magic of her eyes will light the Earth and all things will grow whenever she looks upon them.

And the work of the Goddess will continue, though to most Her Name is unknown; through the one will the knowledge proceed and the Earth will flourish.

And she cries to the Ancient Power a renewal of her oath, that all things will be done, and in the Mother's Name.

And though the foolish fear her name, the work goes on and the secret survives, for the Priestess of the Moon is Witch and all that she is will continue, for without her the Earth would weep and the night would never understand and so would cease to be. She is the spiral of Life — the oceans, the rivers, the falling of the dew. She is the corn at harvest and the birth of birds. She is the wind on the mountain and the spider's web at dawn.

And all things of beauty are Her Name, for she is the reflection of the Goddess of all living things.

And if she could not continue then all hope would cease to be . . .

Introduction

All of the techniques described in Section One, Part One are basic requirements for any self-development training that you could ever wish to follow. Section Two is meant to give the reader some idea of how to experiment and expand upon the basics. The degree to which you can expand is entirely up to you and *no-one* can teach you how far you can, or wish, to go. Whatever you learn is automatically projected into your environment and that in itself denotes change to your basic lifestyle. You may find yourself with little or nothing in common with the people you have associated with for years. You may find yourself in conflict and turmoil, frustrated and daunted at every turn by an inability to accept confines that you, in your past, have created.

So the problem is going to be whether or not to break away from your present lifestyle or to somehow incorporate it. I once knew a woman who pursued an occult path; she had three children and a husband who had been a part of her life for many years. The children were very understanding but her husband kept harassing her for her newly-made associates and spiritual practices. There was all kinds of trouble — fights and walk-outs and slamming doors — he would say she had changed and this wasn't the way he expected her to be, and she would refuse to discuss the matter, saying that he didn't want to understand and was jealous of her new-found feelings and teachings.

There were a few of us at my home one night, including this woman, and we talked about her 'problem' (she hadn't invited her husband, he stayed at home with the kids). We discussed what he believed and what she was learning; she also stated that she didn't want to leave her husband; we asked her if she truly believed what she was following and wondered where the need to argue came from. She said 'He doesn't want me to follow my Path and I'll be damned if I'll let him interfere!' We asked her how he was interfering and she replied, 'He rubbishes me!' We asked how, if she was caring about her family and still following her Path, his 'rubbishing' could have an effect — that if she really wanted to do it then he couldn't stop her, and that only through being who she professed to be could she find peace. Sooner or later if she was loving and laughing and still doing what she felt was right for her, then he would grow to accept and appreciate her.

This is universally true, for only by being what you believe and not by just talking about it do you ever really grow.

Sometimes, of course, there are real problems associated with choosing the Path of the Witch and following it through. It would be foolish of me if I denied that you could run the risk of losing a whole lot more than just your present thought processes. That is why most of us are publicly silent about our Path. The point is that all people have the *right* to choose how they will live their lives.

The hardest lesson in your life could be 'letting go'.

Sometimes there are risks that we take that cannot be avoided. The point is to decide for *yourself*. Don't allow anyone to dictate to you how to seek for truth; start instead by looking within yourself for the answers. Whatever your choice you are going to ultimately affect many people, some of whom you will probably never meet. The work you do (developmentally and ritually) will change your life. *Always* it will change your life.

The thing to be aware of is whether you are using your trained Will to effect these changes or whether you are just 'playing' at training. Many things will occur outside your control; they occur for good reasons. It is not the incidents that matter, but how you deal with them.

Once you have chosen your Path then the effects of that Path or the Energy of that Path will be bestowed upon you from Higher sources and so will the Tests that go with it.

Every human being who lists themselves above the plane of mundane living puts themselves in the Pathway of Inner Initiation. Once you are sure of what you want and this Inner Initiation has occurred there is no turning back; you will quest all your life.

Most people's belief structures are formed at a very young age by the environmental and socio-cultural norms which surround us. Because of the religious structure held as acceptable by both our parents and peers we grow up accepting, albeit apathetically, and relating to the Universe by the decrees set down by others.

Many people remain within these norms and do not find themselves either questioning them or pursuing them to any depths at all.

What is it then that makes some people break out of these structures?

I guess there are as many reasons as there are people who question, but some reasons stand out more than others. One is anger. This anger stems usually from *fear*. People who have been taught to fear the '**Wrath of God**' may become angered at being told that. They may begin to question a God who can cut down the life of a little child for no apparent reason; they may question the rightness of a God who will allow the killing of millions in the name of religion and who will not stop it; one who will wipe out a whole nation through starvation, or who will allow the cruel and arrogant to prosper above and beyond the loving followers of the established religion. On one hand they are being told that God is love and on the other hand they are being told that the same God will cast them into the depths of hell for any transgressions.

If that isn't cause for fear then I don't know what is! What causes the anger is that the followers were fooled into that fear for so long!

Then there is that age-old syndrome — *curiosity*!

Curiosity about how other people worship. Curiosity that demands answers that just seem to always be there. And when they are given they don't always make sense. To ask 'why?' and to be told 'Because it is so!' is not what I would call satisfying.

Then there is that other thing!

A feeling.

A gnawing within the very depths of the self that says 'I know Truth, I just haven't found it within my life.'

Yes! I've heard that one before! There's the breakaway who will not settle for the standards set by others. It's a pre-life knowledge that pursues the individual through every existence. These people will seek their knowledge in 'unacceptable' places. They want to know *enough* to risk the opinions of others, and if they cannot find others who have established groups with which to share their knowing then they are quite likely to form their own.

They are the illumined individuals who are guided from other realms in their pursuit of Truth, and who are driven to pass on to others the knowledge given to them.

All of these breakaway reasons are valid, and seekers after Truth can be found everywhere. The only groups to be wary of are those whose attitudes are hypocritical in practice, or bigoted in their views of others.

Another thing that I find fascinating is the need for people to consider God to be in man's image. Why not woman's? Or a bird's? Or anything else for that matter? Why is it necessary to give form to something that is supposedly Eternal and is supposed to be vast enough to create an entire Universe? To say that God is a man is to endow God-head with the qualities of man and to assume that man is supreme. This is preposterous, and also too limited! I would like to put the proposition that *anything* is God but that the truth of divinity lies with the past and the Centre.

Well then, there you are. There are two definite aspects to

the work and training of a Witch; the first is the discipline of training of the Magical Will through certain tried and true methods, as shown in Part One. The second and most important is the religious training and ritual observance.

As the first section deals wholly with the training techniques which ensure both magically and analytically that weakness and ineptitude do not hamper the 'work' side of your chosen Path, so the second section deals with the real work of the Witch. Part Two has been refined from the *Book of Shadows* to enable the individual searcher to work with the true dedication of the traditionally initiated Witch. To those individuals who can find an authentic Coven through which to train I recommend the manifest form of Initiation to complete the true cycle of 'As above, so below'. There is nothing to compare to the communion of like souls, well trained, working to re-establish the Path of the Absolute Balance at the hand of the Gods, for therein lies the alliance of Light and Dark within ourselves and the world around us.

PART ONE
The Disciplines

Section One
First Stage Technique
Requirements

The Centre

The Centre has been called spirit, essence, soul, consciousness. It is the part of yourself that seeks to know and understand not only who you are but why you are here. It is the gateway to total knowledge.

You are aware that you have five senses: taste, touch, smell, hearing and sight. That part of yourself called the Centre is the sixth sense or inner sight/sensation.

It can best be contacted by considering the other five senses as the perimeter of a circle and all things perceived there flow inwards, literally, to the Centre.

The Centre is also a 'doorway' through which influences not instigated by the conscious mind enter, are assessed and are assimilated into your understanding.

To activate your Centre consciously (because most are already aware of it but this awareness may not be conscious) it is necessary to consider the Centre as also a Watcher. It will use all of your five senses to assess not only how you react to others, but how others react to you; it will take note of what you are spending your time thinking about and will pass, consciously, just exactly what is valid in terms of what you have to say and do and think and feel.

Exercise

Set aside a certain period of each day, for example, between the hours of 6 pm and 7 pm, and consciously be aware of everything that you say, think and feel. Try to pretend that you have an extra set of senses that acts as a camera and recorder, and be prepared to remember all that your Centre perceives during this hour.

At the end of the day when you have some quiet time to yourself recall the things that you were aware of during your designated time and write them down in an order such as:

    what I saw
    what I heard
    what I smelled
    what I touched
    what I tasted
    what I thought about
    what I felt emotionally

If you continue with this exercise over a few days you will find that you are automatically doing it all or most of the time. Remember one important thing . . . the Centre is totally non-judgemental! It is an observer and a conscious purveyor of how you react and act within the known environment of your life. It will be up to you, through your innate understanding of whether you can improve on yourself, to act upon what your Watcher has relayed to you. You may then refine, eliminate or add, as you see fit. Take it slowly as the world has seen too many idealists and perfectionists turn into tortured souls or downright bigots through a lack of scope and an ability, like the Willow, to bend not only to circumstances but ideas and principles that may have been set *for* you and not *by* you!

Meditation

Meditation is a very ancient technique that has been used world-wide by sages, magis, magicians, wizards, monks, priests and people who have in turn learned the technique from them. The actual word 'meditation' is a modern Westernised term for something that does not really require words.

There are degrees or depths of meditation that you will become aware of the more you practise this technique.

If you work on the premise of the Circle again (see Chapter One) then meditation is 'going within' to firstly keep within the bounds of that Circle, and secondly to reach the Centre.

If you stop your reading for a moment and close your eyes you will be aware of a myriad of assorted thoughts and impressions passing through your mind. Try this at intervals during the passing of a day and behold! it is always the same — constant mental activity. One of the most difficult but necessary means of not only coming to know your true Self but of also using that inner knowledge, is through the technique of meditation. Otherwise all you are doing with your time is accruing more and more external data for your mind to sift, sort and categorise.

There are two major reasons for the daily practice of meditation; one is mundane balancing and the other is of a higher nature. (The further you go the more you will merge the two.)

Within the area of the mundane are the daily assaults on your emotions, your body, your creativity and your intellect. Meditation is the art of halting, for a time, these assaults through a positive act of Will. The result should be one of not only coping with these assaults but of riding them with the tranquillity that is within yourself.

It is necessary, within ritual, to be completely centred to enable the work to proceed with intensity. The Centre is like a doorway to things not recognised by the conscious mind. It is your 'power pack' and acts as a lever not only to affect the way you are in the mundane world but as the receiver and transmitter of information and perceptions from other realms of reality.

The act of meditation is almost like a stimulant to aid your Centre to open and close in a more obvious way than it does normally. (*Note:* I did not say 'naturally' as it is natural to have a well-developed Centre and not one that is restricted and constricted through lack of use!)

Do not practise the following exercises in bed as it is likely that you will fall asleep until such time as you are used to the technique.

Exercises
1. Have a very soft, dim lamp or a lighted candle *behind* you somewhere as direct or overhead lighting can be very disconcerting.

2. Seat yourself comfortably either in a straight-backed chair or against a wall with your hands and feet uncrossed. If you are used to sitting cross-legged on the floor with no back support then by all means continue; so long as the pose you take is not a 'fall-asleep' one you will be all right.

3. Begin (with eyes closed) by taking several deep breaths and be aware of breathing by filling your lungs then exhaling totally. Do this if you like by counting your deep breaths. Take no less than ten to begin.

4. Allow your breathing to become unenforced again.

5. The aim now is to allow yourself to drift into the velvety-blackness of non-thought. You will find that your mind will start to work overtime; it will try to trick you into thoughts that enter your mind of their own volition. Use your will to push them out again, gently, always aiming for that state of velvety-blackness and non-thought.

6. Allow just a few minutes the first time, and remember not to apply force against your unwanted thought — just gentle

pressure. The aim is to still your conscious mind. Your Centre is somewhere within that velvety-blackness. When you have reached a state of non-thought you will have reached your Centre, which is a state of tranquillity beyond any you would have at any other time.

7. Allow yourself to drift there as long as you like or as long as nothing interferes. When you have done this, repeat the deep breathing (to rejuvenate) and try to maintain the sense of tranquillity.

Continue this process daily even if it is only for a few minutes — give yourself the gift of making time. You are doing three things:

— disciplining your Will

— discovering the sublime silence at the Centre of your Being and activating that Centre

— caring for yourself

You will find this technique invaluable when you get down to more specific magical visualisation so it is truly desirable to continue and also to begin *all* future exercises with the meditative process.

Visualisation

This exercise is the most important of all for work involved in the occult. I have encountered maybe two or three people in all the years that I have been teaching this technique who were totally unable to visualise. However, they had the ability to conceptualise with similarly accurate results.

Without the ability to visualise projection into the astral realms is almost impossible (at least consciously; it is done unconsciously in the sleep state). The ability to visualise can lead to dramatic changes and accomplishments within your life. Those of you who choose the Path of Magic will find the technique impossible to live without, and those of you who wish to travel to other dimensions will also encounter large problems if you do not master this technique.

The term *visualise* has been described in various ways in many books and by many people. Still there are some who do not think they can visualise (and the same applies to astral projection) because of the various ways that it has been described. The problem that I have faced is one of communication. The word that best conveys the part of the mind that can visualise is *the imagination*. To enable me to do justice to this chapter I would first like to destroy a common myth concerning this remarkable word.

Remember the expression used during early childhood which related to the bridge between the seen and the unseen? Mum or Dad or some other well-intentioned person would say to you, 'Don't be silly, it's just your imagination playing tricks on you!', or 'You didn't see anything there, it was just your imagination!' If you were little and the shadow in the corner of the darkened room scared you it really wasn't much consolation to be told to go back to bed and stop imagining things, was it? Many a highly gifted writer, artist, even mystic or medium may have been deterred from their true Path by that demeaning, belittling expression 'Just your imagination'.

Another common myth refers to an expression I have heard from teachers of the occult, spiritual, mystical and metaphysical Paths when describing how to visualise; 'All you need to do to visualise is to close your eyes and form the picture behind your closed eyes.' And because all there is behind your closed eyes is your closed eyes you throw up your hands in despair saying 'I can't see anything!'

So visualisation is the imagination — but not *just* the imagination. Daydreaming without conscious control is probably the closest you could come to understanding this word. The mind is not so simple a mechanism that it has only one level to its being. There are degrees of depth to the imagination that need as much concentrated study as any other technique. When the required depth is reached then it is possible to stand with the eyes open and see clearly that which you have created with the power of the mind; to activate it to such a degree as to have it appear before you; this is the practice of summoning called 'evocation' rather than 'invocation'.

As the process of meditation is to still the mind whilst relaxing the body, so the process of visualisation is to utilise that peaceful and relaxed state for the creation of new states and increased awareness through controlled and conscious creation.

What begins with the exercise of the controlled creation of a one-dimensional image becomes the creation of a three-dimensional image, then the transmutation of a concept or idea into an image, then in turn to the activation of things and people and the creation of situations that eventually transpire in the realm we call the 'physical'.

From there you will seek through the aid of (1) the Centre, (2) Meditation, and (3) Visualisation to transcend the realm of the physical in search of truths that can only be obtained elsewhere.

There are several exercises to be presented here. If you begin with the first and work it through until it is comfortably accomplished before proceeding to the next, you will find that things move rapidly. Some of you may find the exercises extremely difficult, while others just sail through.

The initial harnessing of the *controlled* image is the important thing to keep in mind so do *not* hurry! (If you are working these techniques with a group then do not let others hurry you either.)

Exercise 1
Go into your meditation. Do some deep breathing and relax your mind and body.
Visualise whiteness as far as your eyes can see.

Onto that white screen visualise a circle. Start at one point on the circle and visualise eliminating it by going around the circle to where you began.

Then recreate it the same way.

Hold the image of the circle exactly as it is for the count of ten, them eliminate it and return.

If you lose control of the image for even a moment do some deep breathing and try again. You may not achieve even this much at your first attempt but continue working at your own pace until it has been done with no interruption from any stray thought.

Exercise 2

Begin with the above until you have the whiteness.

Visualise the circle.

Turn the circle into a sphere which you are to move around in an attempt to see all sides. Note its texture and whether it is of a certain size and colour. If it has no colour then give it some. Play with it a little. Increase its size, change its substance etc.

Hold this scene for as long as you like but stop it consciously and do not allow stray thoughts to interfere. If they do, then begin again or try later.

Exercise 3

Begin with the above until you have the whiteness.

Visualise the circle.

Turn the circle into a sphere.

Have the sphere become a round piece of fruit, eg. an orange.

See your own hands holding the orange. Peel it. Pop a portion into your mouth. Taste it. Chew it. Swallow it and watch it go all the way down to your stomach (if you do not know your anatomy then look it up . . . it must be an accurate visualisation).

Eat the entire piece of fruit following the same procedure.

Again, if you have any stray thoughts enter your controlled

visualisation then stop and either begin again or try later.
Try an assortment of these image creations when you have
mastered the above.

When you have control over your conscious visualisations
then it is time to proceed to the next step: that of creating a
moveable image from an idea or concept.

Exercise 4

Begin with meditation in the usual manner.

Choose a concept. Let me give an example: take the concept of
freedom.

Take the word 'freedom' and try to evaluate its true meaning
for you (not necessarily as may be generally accepted).

Visualise this concept by way of the creation of situations and/
or events to justify your evaluation of the concept. Do not lose
control of the visualisation or allow your thoughts to
wander.

If you lose control then begin again or try again later.

Work on this theme until you have mastered the technique.

From here you will probably have control over all conscious
visualisations anyway so the next step should be childplay!
This involves creation of a fantasy event in which you play a
leading role. Again I stress that you should control it and not
allow daydreaming to interfere.

Exercise 5

Create with the use of the technique of controlled visualisation
an event, featuring people you come into contact with fairly
regularly, in which certain concepts are brought to bear within
that event. Keep it short but ascertain that it is not an ordinary
event like saying 'hello' to George down the street on your way
to work as you always do. Keep it short and accurate and also
keep a note of it written down somewhere. Also, put a time
limit on it, eg. around a week from the day you prepare.

As you can see, not only does this technique require control
and has limitless possibilities, it also requires a certain amount

of responsibility. Bear in mind that if you take the technique to its limits within the realms of the physical then you must also be prepared to bear the consequences of your actions. Don't say I didn't warn you!

Self-Analysis Techniques

I am a firm believer that the human animal and the soul that accompanies it has a unique ability to handle its own life and transcend both the internal and the external problems that assault it.

Here I will begin by offering you another word; this one is crucial in the category of destruction. It is *conditioning*. The majority of problems that are of detriment to our happiness are caused by this word as it rampages its way through our days and nights.

Have a good honest look, for just a moment, at your life as it is right now: the people, things, events around you, and the way they affect you and how you react to them. What you think about when thinking in relation to the individuals both close and not so close to you, and who pepper your life.

How much time is spent dwelling on past events?

How much time is spent dwelling on the future?

There! Hours of time!

We relinquish ownership of our lives to other people so quickly (especially where love is concerned) that the responsibility for what happens to us within the timespan of knowing those people automatically falls on them as if we had no control. Take for example the common expressions 'Look what you are doing to me!' or 'You bastard, it's all your fault!' Why?

When did it occur that another ordinary person was given the power over your life to such a degree? Whatever happened to freedom of choice? Absolutely everyone has the power to change their lives if the way they feel about themselves is threatened by what they feel is happening to them. To lay the blame of your own inability to handle your own emotions upon someone else is to deny yourself the right to a mind, a spirit and the pleasure of living.

An occulist cannot afford to place the control of his/her life in the hands of anyone or anything else and as I have already pointed out the control of one's higher Will is the focal point in training.

Exercise 1

Again choose a quiet place where you are not likely to be disturbed. If you are working the technique alone you will need pencil and paper. If you are working the technique with someone else then they will need the pencil and paper and they will question you and record your answers.

On the top of one side of the paper write 'What I want', and under that write numbers 1 to 20 down the page. On the top of the other side of the paper write 'What I need', and under that write numbers 1 to 20 down the page. Now, out loud start to list the things that you want. You *must* fill in all 20 lines. You may find yourself starting the list with basic material necessities but when you run out of these then go on to the 'emotional' wants.

Don't lie to yourself! If you need more than 20 lines then don't stop until you have exhausted everything. When you have completed this list then begin on the other, that is, 'What I need'. But first cover what you have already written in the first column. As with the above you may start with material needs, then the emotional ones. Again, *don't lie to yourself!* If you need more than 20 lines then keep going till you have exhausted the answers.

Compare the two lists.

Then, having covered the 'What I need' column take another piece of paper with the heading on the top of two columns entitled 'Why?' and go ahead and ask yourself *why* you want what you want and *why* you need what you need. Then consider in all cases what would really happen to you if you didn't get what you want or need. See for yourself how

important the things are to your well-being and happiness if
you do not attain them. If they really are not that necessary
then forget about them and if they really are then set yourself
the goals of attaining them and not just thinking about
them.

Exercise 2
This makes use of what is called the Book of Elements. The
technique is used commonly by occultists and works on the
premise that practitioners will automatically work on any
mundane conditioning complexes that may inhibit their
ability to concentrate upon and control whatever they do
within the context of their Craft.

The technique divides the Self (the Circle) into four
somewhat equal parts (I say 'somewhat' because although
they are considered equal it is always the case that the section
dealing with the emotions takes the most practice to
control).
These equal parts are:

Fire   — symbol of the male principle; deals with
creativity. Represents the conscious mind.

Water   — symbol of the female principle; deals with
emotions, intuition, instinct. Represents the subconscious mind.

Earth   — symbol of the mundane plane and the Earth-
Mother; deals with the physical body and matters of
a physical nature.

Air   — symbol of the spiritual plane and the Sky-Father;
deals with the intellect, the technological and the
spiritual nature of people.

To work the Book of Elements you will first need to

purchase an exercise book and divide the book into four equal parts calling the first section *Fire*, the second section *Water*, the third section *Earth* and the fourth section *Air*. Divide the first pages of each section into two equal parts (down the centre of the page), one side to be entitled *Positive* and the other side entitled *Negative*.

Down the positive side of Fire, for example, you would list all your positive attributes of a fiery nature such as 'I can work on a concept to create' or 'I can create beautiful poetry' — things of that nature. The positive side of the page is for being nice to yourself. The negative side (which the occultist or anyone else is really concerned with) is for weeding out the truth about how we *really* are (and it's no good saying, 'Oh I know that about myself anyway, no need to write it down' because that is a copout!). On the negative side of Fire you would list all of your negative qualities in this area. For example, 'I have a violent temper' or 'I couldn't be bothered to show enthusiasm towards anything'.

For the positive aspect of Water you would put something like 'I am very loving'. On the negative side you would put something like 'I am loving to the point of suffocation'.

For the positive aspect of Earth you might list something like 'I am good with money' or 'I like my body'. On the negative side it could read 'I am tight with everything I own' or 'I am too fat'.

For the positive aspect of Air we could say 'I am very intelligent' or 'I lead a spiritual life'. On the negative side it would be along the lines of 'I am too lazy to improve my mind' or 'I am more concerned with physical and material progress than with spiritual growth.'

There will be thousands of comments that only you can make — really interrogate yourself.

Then . . . see how many of the negatives for Earth, Air and Fire are really emotional and how many of the emotional negatives can be eradicated or transmuted into things other than what they are.

Forget about your positives unless they are really negatives in disguise and concentrate on your problem areas only *after you feel that you have honestly picked them all* and then ask yourself (and write it down) why they are negatives, just what is wrong with them, and even what you feel caused them.

The aim is to get to the Centre of yourself and your motivations and find the big issues about yourself after having eradicated the others and turn the tide on them to aid you in loving yourself.

When you have completed your Book of Elements and have gone over it and over it to see if you can add or subtract anything I suggest you *get rid of it*!

While we allow ourself to be conditioned to expect the woes of others, while we allow ourselves to wallow in a lack of control and self-respect, while we allow others to direct the states of our emotional and physical well-being we are unable to truly develop any abilities of a psychic or occult nature as we are constantly dwelling in a state of tension — under pressure from ourselves. In this state we are forever seeking to please others for their attention or seeking to dominate them emotionally and missing the chances that life may be handing to us through lack of tranquillity.

The Flow Affirmation
One of the most hindering problems that we are faced with constantly is that of getting caught up in situations that confront us. The use of this concept is of benefit on a daily basis, preferably first thing in the morning.

Eventually the actual visualisation technique is to be reduced in value to four words.

The Visualisation
See in your mind's eye the top of a mountain. It is the end of Winter and the snows and ice are beginning to thaw; the snow and ice that formed as the air cooled at the end of last year's Summer and probably the Summer before that and the

Summer before that.The melting snow and ice begins with a trickle that gradually builds upon itself as it wends its way down the mountain and flows into other trickles to form, further down, a raging, mighty river that carries the debris of the season with it as it rushes towards the open Sea.

Wherever water moves there is Life.

Wherever water is still, there is eventual stagnation. The process of evaporation (or spiritual upliftment) is the only process that can prevent stagnation where there is still water.

The oceans upon this planet are the sources of all Life and without them and the free-flowing, never-turning rivers, all Life as we can conceive it upon this planet would eventually die.

Life is like a river, then. It starts off small and as it flows it grows. It carries along on its journey anything that becomes caught in its path. Eventually even the strongest blocks to its flow are worn to grains of sand. Eventually all rivers reach the sea, the Universal Mother from which all Life springs. Then the Sea evaporates and becomes the rain, which can be carried far inland by the wind in the form of cloud and mist to again form the ice and snow at the top of the mountain from where it seemed originally to have come. The water that becomes trapped in wayside pools becomes stagnant and dead at its base but it, too, eventually evaporates, forms rain and becomes the beginning all over again.

A river cannot turn around and go back from whence it came. It must inevitably, eventually end where it began and where it finishes.

To become caught up in a routine that is so unchangeable is to become as stagnant water. Movement and change are Life, but no matter how blocked and routine-bound we may become, it is never permanent; death will make certain of that.

How much more satisfying to remain as the river, to assimilate and carry all that it encounters along its Path!

The Law of Life is change. It is impossible to go against this universal and eternal law — as impossible for the stagnant pool to remain forever stagnant.

Eventually even the highest, iciest mountain peak will release its gifts to the ocean.

Exercise
This is done on waking in the morning. Take five minutes.
Begin by sitting very still.
Breathe deeply a few times.
As you breathe repeat the following within your mind:
'Today
Go with the Flow.
Today
Go with the Flow.'
etc.

Go with it until you feel yourself in a state of tranquillity and willingnesss to flow with whatever life brings you *today*.

The tale of the river can be looked at from many directions and pertains to the cycles of life in more ways than just this, but . . . I'll leave you to think about it.

Section Two
Second Stage Technique
Progressive

Realms of Accessibility

This next section does not always deal with what you would consider logic and common sense. There are techniques here that presuppose your progress and your study and your experience of the exercises given so far.

By 'realms of accessibility' I mean realms or planes that are not of the physical. They are not perceived by the five senses at the perimeter of your Circle but are accessed by the doorway of your Centre only.

None of the techniques that are given here require any form of external stimuli (eg. hallucinogens) and should be accessible if you have utilised true inner control.

This technique requires a sound practical meditative application and strong ability to work at deep alpha visualisation. This exercise is practised today by almost all paths of an occult or magical nature but their original sources are not always known and the ways that they are utilised may vary greatly from tradition to tradition.

The technique is very, very old — as ancient as your chosen Path — and was recorded at the dawn of recorded time.

You may find it useful to actually tape the voyages after reading them through and prior to your experience of them.

There are ten Realms that you will travel through; the first

Realm has four inner Realms through which you must pass before proceeding to the others. The last three Realms are not to be accessed without having travelled all others in succession due to the intensity of their intent.

Exercise
Take the position you have become accustomed to for meditation and visualisation exercises.
Begin with meditation, taking yourself as deeply as possible.
Take your time.
Begin your visualisation by seeing the outside of your Circle.

First Realm: four parts of the Self
1. Visualise within that Circle vast expanses of black space. In the space are countless millions of miles of sheer velvety blackness but way past that is a speck of light.
   Travel toward the light.
   On your way you will pass many floating objects that create themselves only to delude you into thinking you are not going where you Will yourself. (Destination: speck of light). These objects will consist of anything from chairs and tables and houses and people to scientific equations, mathematical formulae, quotes from books, etc. They may be anything that your five outer senses could perceive.
   What you are doing is passing through the dimension of your conscious mind. You need to be aware of this in the background of your voyage due to the fact that, at this stage, you are still within the first stage of the first Realm.
Continue voyaging until you reach the point of light in the distance.
See it, as you approach it, as a vast illumined portal that you are to pass through.

2. When you have passed through the portal you will find yourself standing upon stone steps.

Around you as far as you can see there is only a vast expanse of water.

The only way to progress is to go within the water and merge with it.

Dive into the water and look around.

Begin to move forward.

Become like a fast-moving current within the water and pass swiftly through it.

Observe, at all times, the things within the water. However, allow nothing that you may see to deter you from your journey.

After travelling through the water for a while observe a portal in the distance.

Travel toward the portal.

When you reach it you are to pass through.

3. When you have passed through the portal you will find yourself bathed in brilliant light. There are massive walls to your left and right like a corridor but you can see nothing except the path beneath your feet due to the brilliance of the light around you.

Follow the path.

You will hear a sound like a deep roar (as with a waterfall or thunder) that is continuous.

Follow the path toward the sound.

After travelling thus for a time you will see ahead of you the source of the deep roaring sound; you will see a huge vortex or whirlpool.

4. The initial sensation will be of falling and spinning down a vast chasm. The roaring sound is all around you and you can do nothing else but allow yourself to be drawn deeper and deeper down into the vortex.

Experience the sensation of falling, falling. You need have no fear as you are now travelling through the doorway of your own Centre.

You will appear to have landed in a small chamber that has only one door.

You are to open the door and pass through.

Second Realm: Astral

You find yourself in deep night. The landscape is desolate and barren. The entire field of your vision is lit only by strong moonlight. There is a path at your feet that leads off into the distance straight towards a mountain of rock. You follow the path.

Observe everything as you travel towards the mountain. The path ends at the base of the rock and in front of you you will see a pale wooden door with a lunar crescent made of silver set into it.

You are to knock upon the door and wait until it is opened from the other side.

This is the Gate of the Moon; the doorway that is the entrance of all true Inner Plane encounters.

The door is opened by a woman with dark hair. She wears a robe of silver thread. She says nothing to you but lets you pass into the mountain of rock. You must enter and go your own way for a while, observing everything.

When you have wandered through this mountain and gained whatever information or knowledge is to be found there you will be shown another door by the woman with the dark hair and silver robe.

This door is the colour of the rising sun and you must knock and wait until it is opened from the other side.

Third Realm: First Inner Plane

The door will be opened by someone dressed in an orange robe. The entire place that you have just entered is diffused with a deep red glow. The Being who opened the door to you is more female than male but is definitely a mixture of both.

This Being is both the Master and the Servant of this Realm

and as you progress through this place you must observe and listen to everything. You will be accompanied by this Being who will either tell you and show you many things *or* may choose to tell and show you nothing but leave you to your own devices. Just flow with *whatever* happens until you are led to the next door.

This door is the colour of a wooded glade. You are to knock upon the door and wait until it is opened from the other side.

Fourth Realm: Second Inner Plane

The door will be opened by someone dressed in a green robe. The entire place that you have just entered is diffused with a deep orange glow. The Being who opened the door to you is more male than female but is definitely a mixture of both.

This Being is both the Master and the Servant of this Realm and as you progress through this place you are to observe and listen to everything. The Being will accompany you and may show you and tell you many things *or* may choose to leave you to your own devices. Just flow with *whatever* happens until you are led to the next door.

This door is the colour of the sun at midday. You are to knock upon the door but must wait until it is opened from the other side.

Fifth Realm: Third Inner Plane

The door will be opened by someone dressed entirely in yellow. The place you have just entered is diffused by a yellow glow. The Being who opened the door to you is androgynous.

This Being is both the Master and the Servant of this place. As you progress through this Realm you are to observe and listen to everything. The Being will accompany you and may choose to impart much that is important to you *or* may leave you to your own devices. Just flow with *whatever* happens there until you are led to the next door.

This door is the colour of blood. You are to knock upon the

door and wait until it is opened from the other side.

Sixth Realm: Fourth Inner Plane
The door will be opened by someone dressed in a red robe. The entire place that you have just entered is diffused with a deep green glow. The Being who opened the door to you is more female than male but is definitely a mixture of both.

This Being is both the Master and the Servant of this place and will accompany you *at all times* as you travel. You are to listen to and observe everything. The being may choose to show the things of importance that exist here *or* may leave you to explore and discover without assistance. Just flow with *whatever* happens until you are led to the next door.

This door is the blue of a tropical lagoon. You are to knock upon the door and wait until it is opened from the other side.

Seventh Realm: Fifth Inner Plane
The door will be opened by someone dressed in a deep blue robe. The entire place that you have entered is diffused with crystal-blue light. The Being who opened the door to you is more male than female but is definitely a mixture of both.

This Being is both the Master and the Servant of this place and as you progress through this Realm you are to observe and listen to everything. The Being will accompany you and may choose to show you and tell you many things *or* may choose to let you experience this place without asssistance. Just flow with *whatever* happens until you are led to the next door.

This door is as black as obsidian. You must knock upon the door and wait until it is opened from the other side.

Eighth Realm: Sixth Inner Plane
This time the door swings open without the visible aid of anyone or anything.

The place that you have just entered is diffused with a deep purple glow. Ahead of you is a passageway down which you are to walk. After a time you enter into a vast cavern that has been cut out from the depth of the mountain by unknown forces. The purple glow is everywhere.

At the end of the cavern you will see a Woman dressed in a glowing black robe. She is veiled. She is seated upon a throne which has been intricately carved from the rock within the cavern.

You approach Her and see a silver disc upon the floor at Her feet upon which you sit. She may not choose to speak to you but She is capable of projecting images and concepts into your mind which you would do well to heed. *Forget nothing!*

There is no Servant here. She is Mistress of this Realm.

When She is done with you She will point to a doorway within the wall of the Cavern.

This door is the colour of the stars at night. You are to knock upon this door and wait until it is opened from the other side.

Ninth Realm: Seventh Inner Plane

This time the door swings open through no visible cause. The place that you enter is diffused with a glow that is as white as a pearl and has the same sheen. Ahead of you is a passageway down which you walk.

After a time you enter a vast Cavern which is very bright and which has many high windows that look out onto more whiteness. The pearly glow is everywhere.

At the end of the Cavern you will see a Man dressed in a white robe that is covered with the signs of the Zodiac. He is seated upon a throne which has been carved from the white rock of this Realm. At His feet is a gold disc upon which you are to sit. His face shimmers so that it is impossible to see His face.

He may not speak to you but He is capable of projecting images and concepts into your mind which you would do well to heed. *Forget nothing!*

There is no Servant here. He is Master of this Realm.

When He is done with you He will point to another doorway within the wall of the Cavern.

This door is a swirling mass of all the other colours that you have passed through. You are to knock upon this door and if it is meant that you enter, the door will be opened.

Tenth Realm: Akasha, Hall of Records
The door swings open without visible cause.

You enter into an eternal space that has no colour but only luminescence. As far as you can see in all directions there are Spheres that can be entered into and experienced for what they hold. They are suspended by the force of their own energy.

Within each of these Spheres is a vast library of Knowledge that stretches from Infinity to Infinity; all things that have happened, are happening or will ever happen are contained here.

Who knows? You may enter one of these Spheres that contain all pertinent information directly influenced by your own eternally waking soul!

When you have been there for the required time you must leave.

To do so all you have to do is turn around (where-ever you are standing) and you will find a vortex into which you are to project. This vortex will carry you back to the outside of your Circle and into the realm of the physical.

You may make this journey a thousand times and never receive the same information from any one Realm.

You may enter any Realm through the Vortex after accessing the Gate of the Moon *except* the last three (eighth, ninth, tenth) as these Realms should be entered after having travelled through the preceding doorways and having learned what they have to teach.

Do not go outside the guidelines that have been laid down for you. When you have completed your travels record all

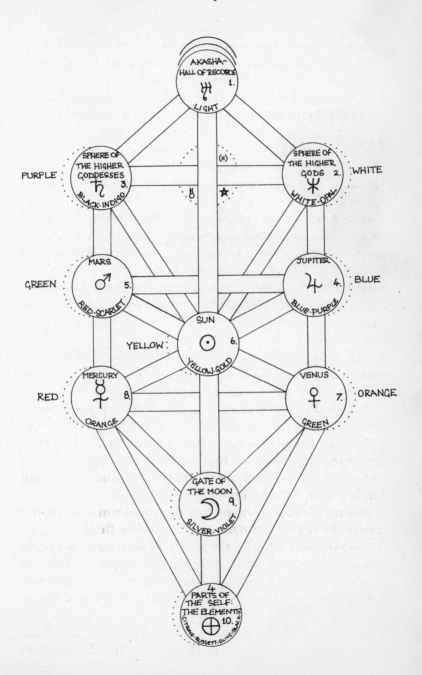

pertinent information in your Grimoir. Do not try to analyse logically the information received, just acknowledge it and be willing to accept it and observe, during the days following your working, the events that occur that may have pertinence to information received whilst travelling the Inner Planes.

Astral Projection
There is a difference between astral projection and astral travelling (or out-of-body experience) and this must be clarified first.

Astral travel occurs whilst in the sleep state and to travel consciously takes years of determined practice that may not necessarily pay off. You would have heard of cases where, at the time of clinical death or within operating theatres, the astral body has taken over the greater part of consciousness. This occurrence is due to the Centre presuming the onset of death.

It has also been known to occur at times of emotional crisis or when an individual is under enormously distressing conditions.

There is an inbuilt fear of death, especially in Western society, which will lead to strong defence controls by the subconscious mind. The latter is the controller, and seeks to prevent any experience resembling that state. The subconscious mind is, however, governed by the Centre which in turn is governed by factors, depending upon the soul's development, derived from the Inner Planes and their requirements of you within this lifetime. To avoid creating trauma in the consciousness of an individual the messages of service received by the Centre will be relayed only as far as the subconscious mind, which will then direct the astral body to travel during the 'little death' known as sleep.

There are differing states of sleep experience:

1. Dreams which break down into symbols the situations happening in your day-to-day life. During these dreams you

may act out parts which pertain not only to yourself but to other people, even objects that have a symbolic interplay. You must understand that your subconscious does not function with the use of words — only in pictures and symbols.

Keep a diary in which you will record all of your dreams and try to interpret them yourself without the aid of books (books may have general merit but they are still only general and the only person who can truly interpret your dreams is you, or someone close enough to you and yet sufficiently unbiased in their knowledge of you for you to trust and talk over the implications of the dream).

2. There are precognitive dreams that may also appear in symbolic form. You will, after becoming aware of your dreams, be able to tell the difference between dream types without any confusion whatsoever. After some practice you will be able to divide your dream diary into sections.

3. There are analytical dreams that pertain to events that have occurred within your present situation. These are 'sort and categorise' dreams whereby you become an observer of a magnificent, computer-like function of the mind. This process takes place at all times but is most obvious during the sleep state as there is no external intake of perceptions that require your attention.

4. Astral travelling; a child dreams of flying, you dream of flying. You dream of strange and wonderful places and people. You have dreams of deep religious and/or spiritual significance. You are given specific information which is relayed through symbolism of your particular Path. You are given tasks or assignments. You derive information from Inner Planes to guide you. You derive information from Akasha on varying subjects, such as past civilisations or the impending course of our planet. Many, many more things. You may find that you are assigned tasks that are to be your

responsibility during this entire lifetime. Much, much more may arise — depending on who you are.

Astral projection is a conscious projection of part of the astral self only. This part is almost like a thought projection, but with more substance. You can be observed by sensitive people when in a state of projection. You can also gain knowledge or information when in this state.

The techniques available for activating the Centre for conscious astral projection are all fairly similar, and all of them work.

You must persevere if you wish to become adept at this technique.

Exercise
The night is the time to practise this technique, as you will require a great deal of concentration. You will be utilising the technique of visualisation but instead of internalising, you are going to externalise your consciousness.

1. Seat yourself in your usual working position and go into meditation to centre yourself.

Visualise yourself standing up directly in front of where you are. Observe the back of your head, your height, your stance — everything about yourself that you can see. It is impossible to observe your own face in this context as we are only aware of our internalised 'externalisation' of image and not the way we look upon observation so to try this would automatically result in failure. (Try anyway, if you like, for the sake of your own curiosity!)

Now . . .

Next you are to project your consciousness into your body. By this I mean to no longer be the person observing but the person being observed. Look around your immediate environment. Go to the doorway and begin to walk around the room observing everything; look behind objects, inside cupboards and boxes, look closely at pictures and books . . . everything.

Continue this exercise nightly until you are familiar with your immediate surroundings. Remember to return to your inert physical body and re-enter the way you left.

2. Begin with meditation.

Go with the process of projecting your consciousness into the image of yourself.

You may now proceed to leave the room that you have been orienting yourself within and travel around the house in which you live, observing at all times and remaining aware of everything which your five inner senses may pick up. If there are other people in the house you may pick up on their emotions etc., but at this stage do not try to have them become aware of your presence. (Any of them may become aware of you anyway, especially if asleep and travelling close to their physical habitat.)

Continue with this exercise nightly until you are familiar with the process.

3. Begin with meditation.

Go with the process of projecting your consciousness into the image of yourself.

You may now proceed to leave the house and walk around outside. Be aware of the time. Observe all about you. Now you may begin the process of expanding your astral consciousness. If you bend your knees and jump you will find that you are weightless and can keep rising as high into the atmosphere as you please. You should also, by this time, be aware that you can 'think' your astral body from one place to another without following a familiar route.

Practise this often. And don't forget to follow the return-to-body procedure!

4. Begin with meditation.

Project your consciousness into the image of yourself.

Have it previously arranged with a close associate that you

will project to their house at a certain time. Anything observed by your associate is to be written down by them and you are to record all that you observe immediately after returning. Firstly it is advisable to follow an approximate route to their house. Drawing a map and committing it to memory is advantageous. Try to fly a route that you would follow if walking or driving.

Come to the outside of their house and up to the front door and either open the door or pass through it, observing everything. Look for your friend and observe. Look for a clock to ascertain the time. Try to pass through your friend's form. Try projecting emotive images . . . try anything that you like!

Return via the same route and return to your body. Record your experiences. The next day talk to your friend and assess any findings.

5. The rest is up to you. Remember the 'truth' factor. If you are 'blocked' from projecting anywhere there is always a good reason.

The degree of your adeptness at astral projection is up to you. Once you have learned the basics then experiment.

Chant and Power Breathing

Each tradition has its own form of chanting — varying from High Gregorian Chant to the Sacred Names of the Gods and the Goddesses. All chants, from whatever tradition, are meant to raise the inner power, or divinity of the Self.

It is possible to raise this kind of power without using any of the known or usual form of chant; using your own name, for example, will raise your energy and will elevate the Spirit. It can thus be used to enhance your 'work', among other purposes.

Exercise 1
Begin with meditation. Allow the breathing to become

rhythmic and sonorous. Allow the breathing to expand into sound (which will begin naturally as a single vowel). Keeping the resonance of the sound, incorporate your name, keeping the chant low and its accent on the vowels the whole time.

Whilst chanting your name see the outside of your Circle and feel the chant drawing you inwards towards your own Centre. When you reach the Centre begin to come outwards again like the ripples on a pool and allow the ripples (your own energy) to progress out past the perimeter of your Circle and spread around you in waves.

After doing this exercise, on each occasion, sit quietly for a while observing your own inner thoughts.

Exercise 2
Begin with meditation. Allow the breathing to become rhythmic and sonorous.

The thing to remember about chanting is not necessarily what you chant as how you chant it. The most important thing about it is that you create a vibration with emotion behind it, and it must be done slowly.

This next exercise must accompany visualisation. A helpful visualisation is to see yourself flying over the planet close enough to the surface to be aware of rivers, mountains, cities, plains, deserts, forests, oceans etc. and chant:
'At One!' and repeat until you are high.

After doing the exercise, on each occasion, sit quietly for a while observing your own inner thoughts.

You can, remember, use anything to chant with and it will raise the concept of what you chant within your Centre and also within your immediate environment.

Take care, then, what you chant but experiment.

Exercise 3: 'The Flier'
This technique is called 'loud breathing'. The inward breath is silent and the outward breath is released with a deep-throated sound.

Begin slowly filling your lungs to maximum each time. Gradually increase the speed of your breaths, allowing the tone to become higher and higher. Allow it to build naturally. If it gets louder and this does not bother you then just flow with it. Let it reach its peak. Then allow your breathing to lessen off naturally unless you are working a purpose, in which case you will hold it at the apex.

Do this as often as you require; it should give you quite a boost. This technique, coupled with chant, is important when working spellcraft and when raising power for any purpose.

Note: When you come to Section Two and involve yourself with the rituals therein you will read the terms 'chant of power' or 'Tantric chant'; this technique relates to those terminologies and you will be at a loss to know what is meant unless you have read and practised this exercise (and read the footnote).

The Mirror
If you find this exercise disconcerting then leave it until you are more certain of yourself.

This is an exercise in Vision — not visualisation but actual Vision. You may find this a very useful tool for the discovery of not only your past selves but also of energies or entities that are around you, both your own and those that you have drawn to you.

Exercise 4
Have a fairly large mirror; large enough to see your whole face and shoulders. Have a candle in a holder.

Rest the mirror either on the floor in front of you or on something that will allow you to see your face and shoulders clearly from sitting level.

Don't wear clothing that is multi-patterned or that will take away from your concentration upon your face (the focal point).

Light the candle and place it on the floor in front of the mirror.

Switch off any other lights in the room so that there is only the glow from the candle. Seat yourself before the candle and go into meditation. Keep your eyes open, focused upon your own eyes in the mirror. Blink when you feel the need. Start by 'pant' breathing and allow it to progress naturally into the chant of your own name. Allow your body to rock backwards and forwards to each chanted word. *Do not* lose eye contact with yourself. If your name chant drifts off into other sounds then let it do so.

Allow the mirror eyes to pull you.

Every now and then interrupt your chant with the words 'I Am'. Watch the faces in the mirror change and vary and just flow with what happens.

If, after a while, you feel the need to close your eyes and just 'travel', then by all means do so.

When you are done, then take some deep breaths and just relax. Conclude the exercise by bowing to your image-self and saying, 'I am who I am and I am One!'

Keep a record in writing of whatever you discover.

Colour
Here I intend to give you some correspondences that can be used to heighten whatever working you attempt. (There is a comprehensive list of associations at the conclusion of this book which you might find of value.)

There are many visual aids that can be used to assist you if you find that you need them, and colour is vibration — along with sound and number. The tool of creative visualisation is necessary with all workings, however, to add Will to intent.

Certain things, through the significance of their use and the constancy of action and intent, can assist you in directing your Will. It is also important to remember that thoughts, emotions and actions that are constant take form and become tangible in the astral realms. Certain symbols, through consistant use, become a universal reality on this plane; so it is with the symbolism of colour.

Certain colours of the spectrum (and beyond, as with black and white) have been used historically by differing traditions to indicate certain symbolic states.

The exercise here is to use your own creative visualisation and incorporate the colours into them. They are also a practical form of raising energy.

CHART 1
Basic Correspondences

RED : Love, passion and will power, also anger and lust, the blood and circulation

ORANGE : Constructive activity, communication

YELLOW : Intellectual creativity and projection of Self

GREEN : Beauty, healing and self-control

BLUE : Aspirations, ideals and justice

INDIGO : Integration and balance

PURPLE : Higher aspiration, inspiration and trans-mutation of egoical desire

CARMINE : Compassion, humanitarian and union with the divine

CHART 2
Astrological Associations

RED : Aries

BLUE : Libra

GREEN : Taurus

SCARLET : Scorpio

YELLOW : Gemini

PURPLE : Sagittarius

SILVER : Cancer

BLACK : Capricorn

GOLD : Leo

TURQUOISE : Aquarius

BROWN : Virgo

VIOLET : Pisces

CHART 3
Planetary Associations

MOON	: Silver	: Astral
MERCURY	: Orange	: 1st Inner Plane
VENUS	: Green	: 2nd Inner Plane
SUN	: Yellow	: 3rd Inner Plane
MARS	: Red	: 4th Inner Plane
JUPITER	: Blue	: 5th Inner Plane
SATURN	: Black	: 6th Inner Plane
URANUS	: White	: 7th Inner Plane
		(also the Sphere of the Zodiac)
NEPTUNE	: Crimson	
PLUTO	: Blue/Black	

CHART 4
Elements

EARTH	: Green
WATER	: Blue
FIRE	: Red
AIR	: Yellow

Number Symbolism

Numerology is the science that concludes that because all things are vibrational they can be reduced to numbers, and that all numbers can be reduced to a single value, 1 through 9 (the exceptions being 11, 22, 33 as significant to the concept of spirituality).

The exercise here is to consider each number and expand upon the concept by putting pen to paper and flowing with what you feel goes beyond; how each conceptualised number pertains to your life both physically and spiritually. I have broken down the meanings of each number to their lowest symbolic denominator.

To relate these concepts to yourself you first need a basis upon which to work so without giving a full layout of Numerology I will summarise that here:

First you write the name you were born with and equate numbers to each letter (see chart). You break the name down to five concepts:

1 The vowels add to: (= Soul Number)
2 The whole name adds to: (= Total Self)
3 The consonants add to: (= Personality)
4 The first letter is: (= Foundation)
5 The number of your 'given'
  name: (= Key to Destiny)

Secondly you take your date of birth and add the breakdown of numbers; this gives your Destiny.

Thirdly you see which numbers need working on; this is attained by noting which numbers are missing from the name or where there is only one of a letter.

Fourth you find the vibration of your personal year from your day and month of birth plus the calendar year of your last birthday.

In the example below, reduce numbers greater than 9 are reduced to a single total by adding the digits together, eg 12 becomes 3, 24 becomes 6. These are shown in brackets

Alphanumeric conversion chart

1	2	3	4	5	6	7	8	9	11	22	33
A	B	C	D	E	F	G	H	I	K	V	—
J	—	L	M	N	O	P	Q	R			
S	T	U	—	W	X	Y	Z				

Example

Name:	Jane	Mary	Smith	
Assigned numerals:	1155	4197	14928	
1. Vowels add to:	1 5	1 7	9	= 23(=5)

2. Whole name: 1155   4197   14928   = 57
   adds to: 12(=3) 21(=3) 24(=6) = 12(=3)
3. Consonants: 1 5   4 9   14 28
   adds to: 6   13(=4) 15(=6) =16(=7)
4. The first letter: 1
5. The number of your 'given' name: 3

Date of birth: June   5th   1922
                     6   5   14(=5) = 25(=7)

Calendar Year: 1966 = 6

Therefore:

Soul Number   = 5
Total Self   = 3
Personality   = 7
Foundation   = 1
Key   = 3
Destiny   = 7
Problem   = 3, 6
Personal Year = 8

It is not necessary to have a full Numerology Chart made up to know who you are; if you feel it important there are many fine books on the subject. This is not the object of this chapter. You are to use the aspects of the numbers to become familiar with the concepts listed below. These numbers have connections with all other aspects of the occult and their union with those factors is what must concern you here.

What you must be cautious about is not to become ensnared in the usage of either Numerology, Tarot or Astrology as an excuse for your shortcomings. Personalisations can be destructive to your goal, which is overall understanding!

Number 1   :   I am
Number 2   :   I share
Number 3   :   I express
Number 4   :   I build

Number 5   :   I change
Number 6   :   I comfort
Number 7   :   I seek
Number 8   :   I accumulate
Number 9   :   I feel

Number 11   :   I accept
Number 22   :   I expand
Number 33   :   We are one

Write your understanding of each concept. Remember that 11, 22, 33, relate to spirit expressed in the physical.

Seek to incorporate each number into your lifestyle.

Planetary Symbolism

There have been cosmological frameworks describing planets since Sumer (with the Ladder of Lights). I have included in the exercises of this chapter a breakdown of hours of work by my friend and 'brother' Bernard Casimir, a humanist astrologer, with some refreshing and slightly unorthodox views on the science.

Apart from the seven planets normally dealt with we have also included Chiron, plus, of course the Sun and the Moon (not true Planets).

Each aspect of each planet has three levels that you are to discover as you proceed with your own learning.

The first step is to consider and relate to all of the aspects mentioned below. The planets are set out in precise order, like building blocks, as life is a series of progressions. This order could be considered as a blueprint to mundane and spiritual development.

I am using word associations in relation to the symbolism of each planet:

Sun   Centre of the Self (symbolism: spiritual flame). Represents your purpose of being within your Destiny. It is the principle of self-actualisation.

It is your Essence and therefore your Will to Be (as in Becoming) and your ability to create and thus express yourself.

Moon
The Moon is responsible for receiving and reflecting the Sun's rays (and light). It is the facility that endows you with your intuitive/psychic faculty, which determines how the energies of the Self are used. It indicates the sub-conscious mind and is also the Mother-image of your Being (that is the nurturing and protecting Self in an emotional context). It endows the instinctive habits of self-preservation.

Mercury
The conscious mind. Mercury endows you with your basic attitudes towards your environment. It rules communication on a contact level (to extend yourself into the environment via communication of your identity). It endows the expression of perceptions with an intelligence through the spoken or the written word. Mercury is the quality of thought, as distinct from the quantity, and the ability to focus thought and direct it outward.

Venus
Venus gives form to what Mercury produces in concept. It is the deciding factor in what you are attracted to or what repels you. It is also that which establishes the essential values in your life. Venus represents your sensitivity and feelings.

Mars
Mars indicates your basic excitations and the quality of initiative and decisive action. It denotes your aggression and your striving

nature. It is responsible for your outgoing sexual nature, and also your tribal affiliations. Mars rules the muscles and all physical energy. It is your powerful aggressive-preservation instinct (the baboon could be considered the symbolic animal of the planet Mars) and it is more social than personal.

Jupiter   This represents your basic capacity for expansion in any given endeavour. It also reflects your ability to improve yourself through education (in this respect it is polarised with Mercury). Jupiter governs ingrained traditional philosophies, from religion to politics. It also pertains to the devotional aspects of the Self.

Saturn   Saturn defines your limitations. It relates to your concrete creative faculties and is the crystallisation of the Sun's energies (the Self). It represents all conditioning aspects, not only within yourself but within society as a whole. It relates to the binding and restricting influences on you. It is there only to give you the opportunity to break through the immobilisation of your own limitations. Saturn symbolises achievement within the acceptable cultural limitations of present-day society.

Chiron   The way through (between Saturn which relates to restriction, and Uranus which influences vision before the action). It is a gateway to spiritual liberation. It is the dissatisfaction that leads to inner rebellion. The Chiron influence is not a quality with which you are born but rather one that can develop through an active involvement in social and cultural affairs — something which endows you with a sense of responsibility other than that which society expects (an underlying need of the collective unconscious). It indicates the 'darkness' prior to 'initiation'. It is the avenue through which you may seek a higher meaning to life which leads thence to a transcendent vision (Uranus). Its emphasis is on the spiritual mind over and above the mundane mind.

Uranus This Planet plus the next two are known collectively as 'Ambassadors of the Galaxy'. Uranus relates to the vision you can have beyond and above your given traditional norm. Uranus is that which breaks down the walls of accepted standards and deconditions the personal ego. It will lead you into situations that will shatter the previously conceived ideas you have of yourself, which have been established by your environmental upbringing. It is the basic urge towards differentiation and independence of spiritual consciousness, and is characterised by the expression 'mental vision'.

Neptune Neptune has been termed the 'Universal Solvent'. Whatever Uranus has destroyed Neptune dissolves. It has a great deal to do with your faith in what is happening when radical feelings are concerned and when changes occur through them. It indicates your basic feelings towards humanity as a whole. Neptune rules mysticism and the need to propel yourself higher than normal restricted thought. It rules the higher feelings and lateral spirituality, and is characterised by the expression 'visionary feeling'.

Pluto   What's left of you after Uranus and Neptune have had their go at you is what Pluto is all about! All concepts of a spiritual nature are pulverised onto a screen, on which is projected your 'new' image. Pluto relates to the transcendence of your life-pattern boundaries. It is the action which is a result of the 'mental' of Uranus and the 'feeling' of Neptune. It is, therefore, the planet of Enlightenment.

You can use these interpretations in just about any way you choose. Meditate upon their significance to you, personally.

Their qualities can be invoked into yourself by techniques of visualisation and by journeying within the Planes.

Tarot (Major Arcana)

The twenty-two Major Arcana of the Tarot are an excellent tool for gauging your mental and spiritual progress. They are also ideal as an aid to trance voyaging.

Their original usage had nothing whatsoever to do with foretelling the future — this just happens to be a consequence of their use. Their symbology and mystical significance is such that people with a developed ability for foresight find them an accurate tool and focus for concentration.

The Tarot trumps are used for what are termed 'Pathworkings', and this indicates their projection from 0 to 21. Just as you would read a book from the first page to the last so it is with the Tarot.

I intend to give the spiritual significance of these cards without referring to their symbolic interpretation. (Traditionally, the Major Arcana are indicated by Roman numerals, so this is so here.)

0	*The Fool*	The thought before the action; prelife; the concept or inspiration or the initial life spark; the Essence.
I	*Magician*	Force taking form; the first primal action; Creation; all things in potential.
II	*High Priestess*	Life unseen; the Mystery veiled; the unknown after the action; primal silence; the womb and all that it symbolises.
III	*Empress*	The result of action; glory in life; growth through action; fertility of thought gives birth to reaction.
IV	*Emperor*	Competence through experience; authority; externalised expression of Will within the environment.,
V	*Hierophant*	Higher guidance; if restricted it is dogmatic and bigoted, if allowed freedom it is spiritual creativity and faith in things higher.
VI	*Lovers*	The crossroads of thought and ideals; the need to choose between higher and lower values.
VII	*Chariot*	Victory of the Self over mundane entrapment; self-assurance through perseverence; the battle of life's trials won, but not the war.
VIII	*Strength*	Inner force through constancy;

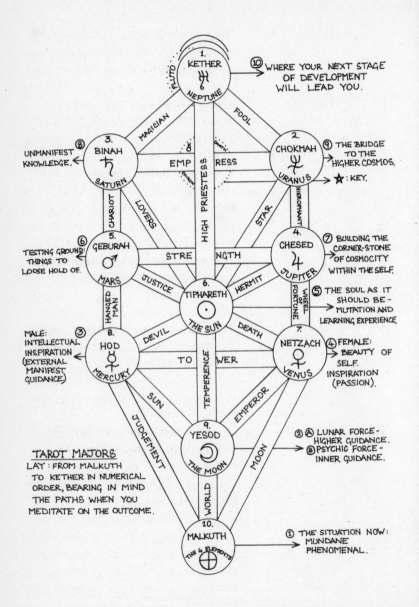

Diagram labels (Tree of Life):

- 1. KETHER — ♅ (Pluto), NEPTUNE
- 10 → WHERE YOUR NEXT STAGE OF DEVELOPMENT WILL LEAD YOU.
- MAGICIAN / FOOL
- 3. BINAH — ♄ SATURN
- ⑧ UNMANIFEST KNOWLEDGE ←
- EMP RESS
- HIGH PRIESTESS
- 2. CHOKMAH — URANUS
- ⑨ THE BRIDGE TO THE HIGHER COSMOS.
- ☆ : KEY.
- CHARIOT / LOVERS
- HIEROPHANT
- STAR
- 5. GEBURAH — ♂ MARS
- ⑥ TESTING GROUND: THINGS TO LOOSE HOLD OF. ←
- STRE NGTH
- 4. CHESED — ♃ JUPITER
- ⑦ BUILDING THE CORNER-STONE OF COSMOCITY WITHIN THE SELF.
- JUSTICE
- HERMIT
- WHEEL OF FORTUNE
- ⑤ THE SOUL AS IT SHOULD BE — MUTATION AND LEARNING EXPERIENCE.
- 6. TIPHARETH — THE SUN
- HANGED MAN
- DEVIL / DEATH
- 8. HOD — ☿ MERCURY
- ③ MALE: INTELLECTUAL INSPIRATION (EXTERNAL MANIFEST GUIDANCE) ←
- TO WER
- TEMPERENCE
- 7. NETZACH — ♀ VENUS
- ④ FEMALE: BEAUTY OF SELF. INSPIRATION (PASSION). →
- SUN
- JUDGEMENT
- EMPEROR
- 9. YESOD — THE MOON
- MOON
- ② Ⓐ LUNAR FORCE — HIGHER GUIDANCE. Ⓑ PSYCHIC FORCE — INNER GUIDANCE.
- WORLD
- 10. MALKUTH — THE 4 ELEMENTS
- ① THE SITUATION NOW: MUNDANE PHENOMENAL.

TAROT MAJORS
LAY : FROM MALKUTH TO KETHER IN NUMERICAL ORDER, BEARING IN MIND THE PATHS WHEN YOU MEDITATE ON THE OUTCOME.

the knowledge that harassment achieves nothing; inner power, outer tranquillity.

IX	*Hermit*	The solitude of one's own becoming; inner wisdom that is unrecognised; spiritual knowledge of one's goals and the apartness that it engenders; no compromise.
X	*Wheel of Fortune*	Situations that cannot be controlled; a testing; higher forces join with those on a mundane plane; reassessment of Self through circumstances.
XI	*Justice*	Following through with an ideal; assessment by higher forces; compassion by the sword; determined awareness; impartiality to external pressures.
XII	*Hanged Man*	True faith in your own beliefs; a demand from within; Sacrifice through higher need of lower demand; the illusion becomes the illumined.
XIII	*Death*	Becoming that which you have strived to become; transformation through initiation; the end of a pattern; the centre of a maze.
XIV	*Temperance*	The new cycle; rebirth; leftover emotional traits bring false dawn;

new ideas surround and influence.

XV	*Devil*	Self-entrapment; the possibility of pompous self-contentment; false and true Knowledge; holding confusion; becoming restricted in spirituality; becoming entrapped in self-righteousness.
XVI	*Tower*	Your own humanity is questioned; circumstances test the determined; if the 'I am' has become the 'better than' you will face spiritual humiliation; your Path is questioned.
XVII	*Star*	Faith illumines the night; knowledge of vast wisdom; tranquillity rewards with both inner and outer beauty; when naked upon the earth plane you are totally free.
XVIII	*Moon*	Intuition brings illumination, though not clearly; acceptance of the wild as well as the controlled; the spirit within is aware of the threat from your lower emotions; acceptance of the primal instinct; illumined understanding of the physical world.
XIX	*Sun*	Inner trust; finding wonder; rediscovery of the nurturing emotion; total individual beauty; knowledge that what you believe

is what you project; simple truth; dawn in the desert.

XX   *Judgement*   Release from darkness; oneness with higher forces; acceptance of 'death' and freedom through understanding.

XXI   *World*   Oneness of Self; the 'flow'; wisdom reveals itself as the spiral; the universal home.

The above are all concepts. There is a spread included to denote your 'place' within present existence and it can be used to ascertain your progress and learning areas.

When you have considered each by way of your own expectations then use each trump in turn as a portal in an inner plane voyage from the base of a mountain to the summit, using whatever archetypes you are comfortable with.

PART TWO
The Way of the Goddess

The Beginning

We stood upon the shore of a great sea. We looked out to the horizon from whence we had come with a longing so painful that none of us could talk about how we felt. Lost upon the shore of an unknown land in the night of a new age with none but ourselves to call upon as friends.

We had been warned; the Oracle had gathered those of us who now stood here and had told us that the Sun had taken toll of the great Crystal and that all was finished. An end to our lands must surely come and the voice of the stars had said 'Go!'

So we took to our boats with nothing but that which we treasured, our Knowledge, our Names and our Inheritance.

Now the Plain lies behind us, lit by strong moonlight. It beckons us to begin the voyage of timeless restoration and so we turn from the longing and the remembering and, one and all, Priest and Priestess alike, set out to fulfil that which has been foretold.

We stand, now, among the Great Stones, and seek through our rites to the Moon and the Sun to bring peace to this ravaged land. The Great Stones shine as once did the Crystal, and the answer comes to the Oracle that much will change but that the seeds of our past shall reach into the distance of time. Further, it is said that what we know will not die but shall be carried within the being of the children of our race, who will be born again and again and again.

The Goddess and the God of the Witch

The primary deity of the Witch is the Goddess. She is known by many names and all are aspects of the one. Almost every culture has at one time worshipped at the feet of the Matriarch.

The three faces of the Moon are the Witch's main concern when seeking to contact Her and work Her Path as Priestess or Priest; these faces are the New Moon, the Full Moon and the Dark Moon known respectively as the Maiden, the Mother and the Crone.

She is, in Her aspect of Earth Mother, known by such names as Dana, Demeter, Ishtar, Inanna, Astarte. She is, in Her aspect of Warrior Goddess, known by such Names as Artemis, Diana, again Ishtar, Nemesis. She is, as Hecate, Goddess of the Crossroads of Fate and Life and Destiny. She is, as Goddess of the Underworld, known by Names such as Persephone and Tiamat. In all Her many aspects She is the Moon Goddess whose worship directs the tides of women, sea and planet alike.

She is called the negative, as a battery has a negative polarity. She pertains to the Earth, the subconscious mind, intuition and instinct, rules the night and sleep and dreaming. She is the *Yin*, the feminine principle, *Anima*. She is the Path of the Incarnate Priestess and the Sister of all women; as such She may be worshipped, revered, adored by all men but by their very incarnate selves they can never really know Her, not as women may know Her. What they can come to know is their own nurturing, compassionate natures, their own intuitive selves, their deeper longing for their own fulfilment through true loving without the need for dominance.

For women, She is their becoming, their strength, their power; She is a universal manifestation of all Women and as such the Priestess is the Goddess if only it be recognised, to pour into our society the force of the female and so to acknowledge the Supreme Mother, Virgin and Whore within us all.

The God of the Witch is also many-faceted and is known by many Names depending upon the aspect one seeks and the reasons one has for seeking Him.

He is the God of Earth and Sky, of Sun and Star. He is aspected in the planets and is the symbol of the seeker in his searching for his higher self as well as the acceptance of the primal side of his being.

He is known as Pan, the Goatfoot God, the protector of plant and animal. He can be seen in all things untouched by the technological mind. He is the primal in all people, and the haunting of the cities by the wild places and the lofty mountains and the deepest forests. As Herne He is the Mighty Hunter, consort of the hunter Goddesses. He is the proud, free spirit of people and nations. He is the wild wind and the mighty beast, He is the Warrior in search of a Name and a Destiny, He is the Stag and the Mountain Lion and the Eagle that rides the currents and tides of the air. He is Apollo, Lord of the Sun, god of truth, healing, the arts and music. He is Ra and Horus of the Sun — also Osiris, consort of Isis and Lord of the Underworld. He is Thoth, god of wisdom and learning. He is Merlin, the great sage and magician, He is Arthur, Llugh and Dionysius, He is Lord Zeus, Prometheus, Thor, Quetzalcoatl, Waken Tanka, Hermes, Janus, Jupiter — and many more.

His most prolific title is Sun God, Master of Magicians.

He is called the positive, rules the conscious mind, the creative and inspirational, the intellectual mind. He rules the day and the conscious, waking state. He is the *Yang*, the masculine principle, *Animus*.

He is the Path of the Incarnate Priest and the Brother of all men; as such He may be worshipped, revered, adored by all women but by their very incarnate selves they can never really know Him, not as men may known Him. What they can come to know is the realms of their furthest intellect, their creative, practical and inspirational selves and their part in the path of transformation of planetary learning without succumbing to the pressure of 'role'.

For men He is their becoming, their inspiration and their wisdom. He is a universal manifestation of all men and as such, the Priest is the God, if only it be recognised.

The Moon and the Sun

As was discussed in the last chapter, the feminine principle is symbolically associated with the Moon and the masculine principle with the Sun.

There are, primarily, two major rituals associated with the Moon and they are the Ritual of the New Moon and Esbat, which is the Ritual of the Full Moon. The third aspect, that of the Dark Moon, is covered in a separate chapter although mention of its purpose will be noted here.

The Full Moon is the time of the Mother. The most productive time of the month to work magic, to invoke forces of a benevolent nature, and the time of worship of the Moon Goddess in all Her aspects. A major part of the working Ritual of Esbat is called Drawing Down the Moon, during which the Goddess in the aspect invoked is drawn into the physical body of the Priestess; during the possession of the Priestess by the Goddess many things may be imparted for the benefit of the Priesthood; foretelling may take place, different techniques of training may be imparted etc. The words of invocation are both poetic and inspiring and the task of fully acquainting oneself with this ritual is the first task to be undertaken.

The Moon, representing the tides, also affects the tides within people and the Full Moon is known as the tide of flux, being at that time of the month when all forces come together as a unit. The actual ritual is all that is necessary at the Esbat, for its primary purpose is one of worship. The feminine principle upon this planet has been sadly neglected in its fullness for many centuries so that, consequently, the balance and order of the planet has been sadly disrupted — an overabundance of either male or female energy creates absolute chaos. We, dwellers on the planet, could not exist if there was no water, no night, no Moon, no darkness — we would dry up, shrivel and die. There has been a tendency historically for an overpowering masculine force since the ideology became entrenched of an all-powerful one-god, male and patriarchal, and this was accompanied by the subsequent subjugation of women. The balance tipped to the side of war, greed, ownership, power for power's sake, bigotry and anger, through the suppression of the compassionate, intuitive nature. The destruction of culture, learning, freedom, wisdom and love through the above disintegration of the strength that is woman has led to a violent suppression of emotion — both in women and in men.

The release of this imbalance has most assuredly begun, and this not only liberates women from the role of subjugation into their true path of power but has allowed men to once again lose their stereotyped role-play in favour of honest emotion. However, we still have a long way to go.

Through its energy, the Ritual of Esbat releases the vision of the Goddess into the Astral and thereby permeates the Universal Unconscious with the beauty of its intention.

The New Moon is intended for the growth of new endeavours. That which is begun at this time can be seen in its completion at the Full Moon. It is the time of the Maiden, the Virgin (which means 'owned by no man') and as such much spell-working is done at this time; those things which need time to reach a satisfactory completion; all things 'planted' at the time of the New Moon grow stronger, faster, than at any other time. Its purpose, as shall be seen, is also for the balance of the Four Elements within the Self and the environment.

The waning and subsequent Dark Moon are used for times of inner seeking and assessment. This time is the quietest for most as the only outgoing workings are those of bindings and protection, where danger is known to threaten. They are *not* times of attack as the tenet of 'so long as ye harm none' applies in all cases where magic is performed, but are times, in need, of defence. At periods of personal crisis, or upon sincere request, the aspect of Hecate, Goddess of the Crossroads, is invoked to aid in a direct passage through trial. Be warned that the invocation of this Goddess (as with Nemesis) must *only* be undertaken during times of dire peril as She is both swift and direct in Her action and should you choose to invoke Her without true need She is apt to turn on you and the full force of your request will rebound on you threefold!

The Sun, in its symbolic form, is associated with the masculine principle.

The major rituals of worship to the Sun God are performed but four times in the year at the Solstices (when the sun is at greatest and least) and the Equinoxes (which is when daytime and night-time are equal).

The invocation of the God of the Witches takes place during the Rite of Esbat and also at times of special need or significance (as for the manhood ceremony for a boy of thirteen years). It also occurs during the four Fire Festivals. His assistance is needed in the making of talismans and His planetary essence is invoked at such times.

The Four Elements

The Elements are both a protective and a balancing factor in witchcraft.

As has been noted in Part One, their importance in self-training by way of the Book of Elements is vital to the properly trained Witch, as a lack of balance and control can threaten any 'work' that may be undertaken.

The Elements are four in number and interweave themselves into Astrology, Numerology, Tarot, Hermetics, Alchemy, Qabalah and Witchcraft alike and all interweave themselves with each other. They are:

AIR   Key factors are East, sunrise and autumn. Air is male/female, its ritual tool is the Athame or Sword, its Elemental is the Sylph and its symbol is

EARTH   Key factors are South (Southern Hemisphere),*
             midnight and winter. Earth is female, its ritual
             tool is the Pentacle, its Elemental is the Gnome
             and its symbol is

WATER   Key factors are West, sunset and spring. Water is
             female, its ritual tool is the Cup, its Elemental is
             the Undine and its symbol is

FIRE   Key factors are North (Southern Hemisphere),*
             midday and summer. Fire is male, its Ritual tool
             is the Wand, its Elemental is the Salamander and
             its symbol is

* These ascriptions are reversed in the Northern Hemisphere.

When working ritual the Elements are invoked as both Watchers and Protectors of the Rite. The winds carry the work to the four corners of the planet and when out of balance there are certain rituals invoking the Elements of Opposite to counteract the imbalance within the self and the environment. There is a chart of correspondences at the end of Part Two which serves as a reference for the necessary associations.

The Ritual of Balance requires that you work respectively through the Elements, allowing a fortnight between, and record your vision pertinent to each in your Grimoir.

I must explain that for your own discipline it will be necessary for you to acquire two good quality diaries each without dates and with plain paper. One is to record rituals and the other acts as a personal record of such things as pertinent dreams, workings, correspondences and all things relevent to the Craft that are of use. One is called a Book of Shadows (ritual) and the other is called a Grimoir (personal record and workbook). All information within the pages is to be hand-written for the express purpose of imbedding the information deeply within your mind.

The Ritual of the Four Elements
Begin with the Element through which you naturally work, eg. *Aries:* Fire, *Taurus:* Earth, *Gemini:* Air, *Cancer:* Water, etc. and work through them.

Each Element has its opposite and this is to be utilised to centre yourself at the completion of the ritual.
For the Rite of Fire:
You will need a red candle, a red cloth for your Altar, incense of either olibanum, wood aloes, oak moss, myrrh and/or cinnamon or mixtures of any of these (if you find it difficult to procure hand-made ingredients then stick to joss sticks of musk for the Rite of Fire).

Choose a night of the waxing Moon. Bathe with the intent of purification. If you have already procured a robe then by all means wear it and if not then wear plain, clean, unencumbering clothing.

Set your Altar in the North.

Lay your red cloth on the Altar and set the candle upon it along with the incense. Light them.

Cast a Circle about yourself in a Sunwise direction calling forth the Goddess and the God by the names that feel right for you to protect you within your Circle.

Stand first to the North and invoke the Guardians of that place to act as Sentinels to your work by raising your right arm and calling:

'**Come Ye of the North Wind, Place of the Highest Sun! Guard this place, set outside of Time, guard this Circle invoked in the Names of the Mistress and Master of Magic and give your aid to my Rite!**'

Repeat this to the other Elements, moving in a Sunwise direction, giving to each quarter the titles of South Wind, Place of Midnight; West Wind, Place of the Setting Sun; East Wind, Place of the Rising Sun.

Seat yourself in front of your Altar to the North and begin with deep meditation using a humming chant on the outward breath to focus your energies towards the candle and thence on out to the North.

Concentrate on pulling the colour red through your body and out into your aura, and consider all things pertinent to the Element of Fire, remembering that this Element relates to the Creative Force and Higher Intellect in its *positive* aspect (as well as such things as warmth, light, sunshine, etc.) and in its *negative* aspects to such things as war, anger, fire out of control, power without compassion etc. Consider as many things as your mind can conceive relevant to Fire, and then bring the colour permeating your being into a thin line down the centre of your body and invoke to the Elementals (Salamanders) of that Realm the following:

'**Ye Guardians of the Palaces of Fire, I seek the pure creative balance of your Force!**'

Repeat three times.

Go into deep breathing and project the colour back towards

the candle where it will be absorbed. Then focus your visualisation, seeing before you a red door with the symbol of Fire upon it. Knock, enter and voyage through that Realm remembering all that you can for later recording in your Grimoir.

When this is done do some deep breathing and feel the cooling energy of rain wash around and through you to balance and ground you.

Thank the Elementals of Fire for their assistance in your work.

Stand to the North and say:

'Ye Sentinels of the North, I give Thee thanks for attending my Rite. I bid Thee go within Thine own Realms knowing that my allegiance is with Thee!'

Repeat farewell to the other directions.

Then give thanks to the Goddess and God and banish the Circle. Snuff the candle.

Record your information in your Grimoir.

Repeat the Rite as many times with the same Element over the next fortnight. Wait again for the waxing Moon and, using the colour blue, repeat for the East. Again at the next waxing using the colour yellow, repeat the process for the South, and the colour green for the West, each time invoking the Elementals thereof. Concentrate on both the positive and the negative attributes of each Element before aligning the balance within, seeking behind the door and symbol representative of the Element the information that awaits you.

It is important to remember the grounding that is obtained from invoking the opposite at the time of balancing, eg. for Fire the cooling influence of rain; for Air the richness of earth and green growing things, for Earth the high mountain winds, and for Water the warmth of a hearth fire.

The Working Tools of a Witch

The first four tools are conceptual rather than actual but are primary if effect is to be ascertained and if your purpose is to register within the higher echelons of the inner planes. These tools are 'to will', 'to know', 'to dare' and 'to keep silent'.

To Will

In its lesser form, the Will of a correctly trained Priestess or Priest should be capable of directing their lives to their satisfaction and likewise for their higher benefit and that of evolution. In its greater form, the Will should be capable, in rare circumstances, of directing the course of events beyond themselves — eg., environmental destruction (man-made) or in cases of threat, either personal or planetary. In all cases the energy raised is for **defence** rather than attack.

No magical tool of a material nature can be charged without the power of the disciplined Will; no circle can be cast, neither can it defend the individual; no elements can be invoked and the Gods, most definitely, remain only the figment of myth.

The list is seemingly endless. Therefore, although initiation may be considered acceptable prior to the development within this work, it is your personal and imperative responsibility to attend to the discipline of your own Will and to consider it as foremost in your self-training.

To Know

Apart from the nature of things that interest you generally it is important that you accumulate as much knowledge of a diverse nature concerning the occult path as you can, as there is power in knowledge for its own sake. All manner of related subjects can only assist you in your work — things of an anthropological, religious, philosophic nature, works by other known occultists, material pertinent to affirm what you learn, ie. astrology, numerology, tarot, hermetics, qabalah, witchcraft, magick, herbalism and the healing arts in general, mythology, legend, history, general science etc.

With all the information that you receive it is important that you take time to put the qualities of your own mind into action to enable you to ascertain the difference between what is purely hearsay on the part of the authors concerned. All things are to be analysed and should lead to a balanced viewpoint based on your own judgement.

No knowledge is ever wasted and it is necessary to know enough to trust your own findings. Ignorance is *never* bliss, and all material viewed can only extend your capacities of Mind.

The material you employ that directly affects your Craft is to be learned and learned and learned so that natural flow occurs which allows other factors of a natural kind to enter into your work.

To Dare

Assuming you have done your work with self-training, and begun disciplining of the Will, you will now be in a position to experiment with what you have learned. You may find it beneficial to read to the end of this material and so have all the information at your disposal before you take on the challenge of daring, but here is the first stage of the material you will employ for the entry to your Grimoir.

Refer back to the chapter dealing with visualisation and look to the last part whereby you create an event of an outside nature. In context with that work we dealt with the mundane only. However, having decided to take up a magical path, you are now to centre your skills on the use of ritual and seek to serve by way of experimenting with the forces around you. Take heed to interfere in no area that does not personally concern you at this stage and where all acts of spellcraft are concerned do not exceed your own ability — to do so would doom your work to failure and waste power of an astral nature.

Say *nothing* to anyone of your experiment, as that also would doom it to fail.

To Keep Silent

In all things this is a very important and necessary function. Unless you have absolute faith in the person with whom you wish to discuss your Path, then say nothing. Personal experience has taught that unless your 'cup is full' you will only deplete what you wish to store by tossing it around, and always remember the world is full of scared, bigoted people.

You will take the essences of the rituals herein and mould them to your own sight and then write them up accordingly within your Book of Shadows. You should treat that Book as sacred, sharing the material with no-one unless they are prepared to follow the same path, for you are working with the Gods and they will not be profaned!

The material that you find works for you may not work for anyone else and again is to be kept silent once it is considered acceptable and has been added to your Grimoir.

Remember . . . never boast, never threaten. Acts of spellcraft are a thankless business due to the very fact that if you discuss them with others they do not come to pass as they are reduced to the boundaries of the mundane, and if you tell of them after they have worked few will believe you in this sceptical world anyway. The times you will have acknowledgement of your undertakings will be if you come to find like-minded people in a coven structure with whom to work. Nevertheless where you find others who wish to form a working group with you, be careful and discerning, as there are those who would suck you dry of all you have learned and then leave for the gratification of their own power. There are also many who will seek power for the sake of power itself, and they are those who endanger the Goddess and Her Children and would abuse the gifts She bestows.

Therefore, speak not of what you know at all until you *become* that which you seek to serve!

The Athame

This is the Witch's main tool of ritual. It is preferably hand-made of iron but if this is not possible then take care to search long and hard to find any material which you deem suitable. The hilt is to be black and the blade magnetised prior to each use. It is the tool of 'extended' Will and as such takes on your own emanations.

The Athame is used to invoke the Elements within the Sacred Space, to cast the Circle, to consecrate all new items within the Circle that are for ritual use.

When not in use, the Athame is to be kept away from the presence of any other person and is to be well oiled, wrapped in either silk or fine linen and hilted in a natural material of your choice.

The Athame is *never* used to draw blood.

The Ritual of Consecration of the Athame

First gather together wine, salt and water in small containers, a cup (if you have not as yet procured a sacred cup then use a glass or goblet), some essential oil, a white candle and incense.

Place all these things upon your Altar.

Bathe with intent of purification.

Wear your robe or, better still, go naked to your Circle.

Light the candle and incense and seat yourself before the Altar with the Athame within your hands and go into meditation. When you are sufficiently prepared then stand and cast the Circle as is described in the chapter on the Elements, then call forth the four directions.

Return to the Altar and raise your Athame high and call forth the Moon Goddess in as many aspects as you can and ask that She bless the Blade of your Art (use your own words which you will later add to your Book of Shadows).

Draw the shape of a pentagram over the Athame saying:

'**I invoke the force of the Mighty Ones to consecrate and** charge this Blade with Universal Will!'

Draw the sign of the pentagram over the salt and say:
'Blessings upon this crystal of the Sea forced from the Womb of the Mother by the might of the Sacred Sun!'

Draw the sign of the pentagram over the water and say:
'Out of Thee, water creature, goes all that is not pure. May only the essence of the Great Mother remain!'

Add the salt to the water and draw the sign of the pentagram upon your forehead with it saying:
'I work my Rite as Priestess (Priest) of the Ancient Way. May the Gods see that which takes place here and give blessings upon my Path!'

Work the salt and water into the Athame, blade and hilt. Take the oil in front of you and draw the sign of the pentagram over it saying:
'I consecrate Thee, oil of the purest plant, mayest Thou aid me in my task.'

Work the oil into the Athame, blade and hilt. Take the wine in the cup and draw the sign of the pentagram over it saying:
'Thou art blessed, fruit of the Earth Mother and the Sun!'

Work the wine into the Athame, blade and hilt. Now take the Athame within both hands and hold it over the candle flame saying:
'The Element of Fire infuse my Blade!'
Over the water and salt saying:
'The Element of Water infuse my Blade!'
Over the incense saying:
'The Element of Air infuse my Blade!'
Then place the Athame, blade down, upon the ground

saying:
    'The Element of Earth infuse my Blade!'
Place your Athame upon your breast and close your eyes, concentrating all of your Will into it. Having spent ample time doing so then say:
    'Thou art Mine! I am Thine! We are One!'
Kiss your newly consecrated Athame, Blade and Hilt and place it upon the Altar.

Now take up the Cup of consecrated wine and raise it skyward in silent homage to the Goddesss and drink of it. Keep some within the Cup to pour upon the Earth in libation after you are done.

Now take up your Athame and dismiss the Elements with it and banish the Circle.

Before putting the Athame away rub the magnet down both sides of the bade. Repeat this process prior to and after working.

The other tools you will need are:

— A **White-hilted Knife** for such things as carving sigils upon candles, cutting herbs for use as incenses, making other tools etc., and it may be used both inside and outside the Circle. This tool is also to be consecrated but whenever the sign of the pentagram is made you will use your Athame. The consecration of this and all other tools is a simpler version of the consecration of the Athame invoking the Gods and blessing them with the salt, water and the Elements.

— A **Pentacle**, to symbolise the Earth. This is a circular disc made preferably of copper. However, wood, wax or even parchment can be used if copper cannot be procured. The main design to be drawn upon the surface is the pentagram and you may add any other sigils of your personal choice. It is to be buried in the path of the waxing moon from New Moon to Full to take within it the Earth emanations of the Moon and is to be consecrated on the night of the Full Moon.

— In Witchcraft a chalice or goblet is used as a **Cup** and is the symbol of Water and the Goddess. This is also consecrated on the night of the Full Moon and is dedicated to the Goddess in Her aspect of Mother.

The Cup is best if it is cast in silver; however, this may not be possible and whatever 'goblet' shaped vessel you can obtain should suffice.

— The **Wand** is, traditionally, carved by hand and this is a *must*. May I suggest the branch of a Willow, as this is soft enough to be easily carved? *Do not* cut the branch when it is still living as this is a brutal infringement of your tools and your pact is to the Goddess of all living things.

The Wand measures from the tip of your middle finger to your elbow and its carvings are to be synonymous with your Art. It, too, is consecrated on the night of the Full Moon but is to be dedicated to the God and is to be considered a masculine symbol, as it is the symbol of Fire. (Other sacred woods include hazel, rowan, oak, elder.)

— The **Cords**. There are two main Cords that are used. The first is a white cord that should be long enough to encompass your Circle and should be kept for that purpose only. The other is to be green if you are a woman and red if a man. This Cord is used for working certain spells and for each operation a knot is tied and remains there.

The most commonly used technique for forming a perfect Circle, if one is outdoors, is the 9-foot Circle formed by sticking your Blade into the Earth and looping one end of the Cord over it while scribing a Circle, at the full 9-foot length of your Cord (pulled tight), using your white-hilted knife to mark the perimeter.

A Witch works naked (or sky-clad) as often as is possible as there is nothing to inhibit body magnetism or movement. The **Robe**, however, is considered as part of your ritual requirements and it may be of any plain colour and any design of your choice but is *not* to be of synthetic material. The Robe is to have *some* hand-stitching on it, done by you, as a symbol of intent. The Robe is donned only within the Circle or the Temple as a symbol of taking on the garb of your Priesthood.

Other items of special significance may be acquired as you go, such as the thurible (incense burner), candle holders, special containers for water and salt, cloths for the Altar, containers for oil etc., but the most difficult of items to procure, and one of the most powerful, is the Sword. In all matters, other than those which I am not permitted to disclose, the Athame will suffice.

The Ritual of the New Moon

The time of the New Moon is the time of preparation and planning for any work that requires patience. As with planting seeds there is a gestation period necessary for natural growth, so it is with many workings that you may undertake.

I have found on several occasions that it has been necessary to seek a new house during the Dark of the Moon and I have always performed a house-finding spell during that time, with the purpose of procuring it by the time of the New Moon. Beautiful houses have always turned up by that time!

The New Moon is a time for honouring the Virgin within Nature — the Wild, the untouched, the untainted. It is the time of giving, when the worship is specifically to raise power for the spirits and Elementals to use in their never-ending fight against the greed and avarice of selfish people on the planet.

The Ritual

Prepare your Altar with the four white candles (to symbolise the three phases of the Moon plus the Altar candle) with three behind the one. Have Incense, Cup, Athame, Wand, Pentacle and red or green Cord plus a bowl of salt and one of water. Also have a small container with earth in it. Have with you a potted plant which you are to have bought prior to the Rite with the express purpose of planting it in some 'hurt' part of your environment.

Bathe with intent of purification.

Use your white Cord to formulate a Circle on the floor around your working area, light candles and incense and seat yourself before the Altar.

Begin your meditation and go from there into a soft chant, visualising the sliver that is the New Moon's first visible appearance.

When you have centred yourself then stand with your magnetised Athame in hand and, starting at the East, move Sunwise around your Circle as you have learned to do raising your Athame blade high in a spiral motion until you hold it directly above your head.

Invoke the Elements as usual.

Return to your place in front of the Altar.

Consecrate the Water and pour half onto the little plant.

Consecrate the salt and add it to the Water. Draw the pentagram upon your forehead with the Water in self-blessing whilst calling upon the Virgin Goddess to come and bless the Rite as follows:

'Enchantments Queen, potent Sorceress of the Crescent Moon, foresee this Rite and aid the Legions of the Elements to restore life where life has been destroyed!

Let not the madmen call the tune!

The Children of the Earth reach out to the Wild, Free Lands and the forces that seek to retain them and pledge their alliance!

O, Virgin Child of Sunset, Wild Mistress of the Hunt, Artemis of the Mountains and Aphrodite of the Seas send Your powers to aid me here!

Your Power I Invoke To Aid Me Here!'

Raise your Athame high above you and raise a chant of power.

While the fullness of the chant is upon you touch first the Flame with the point of your Athame, then the Incense, then the Earth in the container, and then the Water.

Stop at the height of the chant and visualise the forces of each Element's essence. Lift to the top of your spiralled Circle, and shoot them out to be used as a stream of ever-waxing power by the spirits of the Elements. Then say:

'As the mounting tide of the Moon waxes to Full may also the forces of my spell grow. As this tiny plant grows to its fullness may the tide of destruction upon this planet that threatens all life fade and die!'

Thank the Goddess for attending the Rite, thank the Elements for standing Sentinel and bid them return whence they came and banish the Circle. Remember to magnetise the Blade of your Athame before putting it away to keep its purpose active. Before you put your red or green Cord away tie a knot in it to signify a working completed.

Put all ritual things away out of sight before you do anything else!

The Ritual of Esbat (Full Moon)

For the Esbat you will require the following:
Wine; Salt and Water; Cakes (see mixture at the end of this chapter); Cords, Incense, Wand, Athame, Pentacle, Cup, Essential Oil of a type befitting the rite, eg. Jasmine, Rose, Geranium, Camphor, Ylang-ylang or Lotus oil (have some already added to a container of olive oil in your bedroom for self-preparation prior to the Rite.); Four candles for each point of the compass and one for the centre of the Altar.

Prior to the Ritual you are to bathe with the intent of purification and, when dry, rub yourself liberally with the oil. You are to wear no jewellery or clothing into the Circle that is not consecrated and it is best to work sky-clad is the weather permits.

The Ritual

Light all candles and the Incense and close the Circle.

Seat yourself before the Altar and begin with meditation raising a soft humming chant to centre yourself.

When you are ready then stand and raise the Circle:

'Great Mother and Lord of the Skies let your Power raise a Circle of Sanctuary about this, your Priestess (Priest). Let nothing impure enter Herein. May it protect and contain all within its Boundary. This I call in the Names of the Powers of Life!'

Invoke the Guardians of the Elements:

To the North (Fire):

'Come Ye of the North Wind, Place of the Highest Sun and guard this place, set outside of Time, guard this Circle invoked in the Names of the Mistress and Master of Magic and give your aid to my Rite!'

To the East (Air):

'Come Ye of the East Wind, Place of the First Sunrise and Rise of the Moon and guard this place, set outside of Time, guard this Circle invoked in the Names of the Mistress and Master of Magic and give your aid to my Rite!'

To the South (Earth):

'Come Ye of the South Wind, Place of Storms and Deepest Night and guard this place, set outside of Time, guard this Circle invoked in the Names of the Mistress and Master of Magic and give your aid to my Rite!'

To the West (Water):

'Come Ye of the West Wind, Place of the Setting Sun and home of the Island Remembered and guard this place, set outside of Time, guard this Circle invoked in the Names of the Mistress and Master of Magic and give your aid to my Rite!'

Kneel before your Altar and draw the sign of the Pentagram over the salt with the Athame and say:

'Blessings upon this crystal of the Sea forced from the womb of the Mother by the might of the Sacred Sun!'

Draw the sign of the Pentagram over the water with the Athame and say:

'Out of Thee, water creature, goes all that is not pure. May only the Essence of the Great Mother remain!'

Place wine into the Cup and put your Athame blade therein and say:

'The Cup is the Symbol of Woman and the Goddess. The Athame is as Man and God; co-joined they are the blessed union that produces the three drops of Inspiration, the Creation Continuous!'

Sprinkle the consecrated water over the cakes and sprinkle the wine over them also.

Take the water and sprinkle it around the perimeter of the Circle. Raise wine in both hands in honour of the Goddess and drink. Take the essential oil in your left hand and your Athame in your right hand and draw the sign of the Pentagram over it saying:

'Thou art the Essence of Blessing; whereupon Thou touchest all is blessed. Thou art the healing oil, the balm of the Initiate and the juices of the Sky Goddess! Mayest Thou aid me in all things Sacred!'

So doing, stand and place a little of the oil on your finger.

Touch both your feet with oil saying:

'Blessed be these feet made to walk the Path of the High Gods!'

Touch both knees with oil saying:

'Blessed be these knees meant to kneel at the Altar of Infinity!'

Touch the genitals saying:

'Blessed be this womb (phallus) without which no thing is born!'

Touch the breasts with oil saying:

'Blessed be my breast formed in beauty (strength)!'

Touch your lips with oil saying:

'Blessed be these lips made only to speak the Sacred and Divine Names of the Lady and Lord of all Living!'

Then raise your arms out from your sides and spread your legs to form the living shape of the Pentagram and say:

'Five are the points of fellowship, here whence Lance and Grail unite! And feet and knees and breast and lip!
Here the Gate of the Universe wherein all things abound for the glory of the Spiral Dance of the Cosmos.
Thou who art Eternal Queen with horn of Moon thrice crowned,
See here the Child of the Star-Born, we are one with Thee, Thou art One with us!'

Then take the Wand and raise it high saying:

'Thee, I invoke, Lord of the Sun! Send Thine Essence into this Sacred Space to aid in the Rite of the Full Moon!'

Wait until you feel the Power within the Circle then place the Wand upon the ground at your feet and say:

'Giver of Life, Giver of the fruits of the Earth, Witch Lord, Herne, call unto this place the spirit of She who is Queen of all Women, Mistress of all Witches!'

Extend your arms out and up, and with your Will proceed

to Draw Down the Moon. Breathe deeply and visualise a stream of force entering into you from the Moon's Light, the Essence of the Goddess then say:

'She is the Beauty of the green Earth
And the White Moon among the Stars
And the Mystery of the Waters
And the Desire of the Heart of Man!
Call unto Her Soul, arise and reach unto Her
For She is the Soul of Nature Who giveth joy to the Universe.
From Her All Things proceed and unto Her All Things must return.
Before Her Face, beloved of Gods and Men, let thine innermost Divine Self be Unfolded in the Rapture of the Infinite.
Let Her Worship be within the heart that rejoiceth,
For behold, all acts of Love and Pleasure are Her Rituals!
Therefore let there be compassion, honour and humility, Mirth and reverence within us all.
And thou who thinkest to seek for Her, know that thy seeking and yearning will avail thee not unless thou knowest the Mystery.
She hast been with thee from the Beginning and She is that which is attained at the end of all desire!'

Then seat yourself before the Altar and break the cakes and, saving some for libation, eat and drink the wine to the glory of the Gods.

Any 'work' that you had planned is then to be done, eg. healing, scrying, special workings, talismans of significant Lunar importance etc.

At the conclusion of the Rite recite the following:

'Great Goddess of the Moon, let your servants be many and secret. Man is ever a Star and Woman a Moon.
We will rejoice in the Life Universal!

All sorrows are shadows that pass and are done
And always Life remains.
The Truth is the foundation stone of our Art.
So fear not at all neither men nor fates nor anything!
The Great Mother is always our refuge.
I may enter the Circle with a heavy heart but with mirth do
go forth
And with thanksgiving do pleasure on Earth
And give my aid to the legions of the living!'
   Bid farewell to the Elements and banish the Circle.

The recipe for the Ritual cakes is simple:
1 cup of wholeflour
1 tablespoon cinnamon
1 tablespoon honey
¼ teaspoon baking powder
pinch salt
Enough water to make into a cake consistency.
Mix well and bake until done.

The Ritual of Dark Moon

The Waning Moon is from Full Moon to New, and the Dark Moon is the last three days prior to the New Moon when the Moon is not apparent at all.

This time is reserved for working on the parts of the self that inhibit your abilities. Fears are to be faced and overcome using the energy of the Dark Moon; the Shadow is to be hunted and allied to the self and worship of the aspect of the Crone or Dark Mother is to be performed ritually. I know of many people who will not touch magic at this time of the month but that is due to their non-confrontation of the fears that are part of everyone's makeup, especially those who deal with the occult and with unseen forces. It is preposterous to take on the Path of a Witch without working at overcoming fears of such things as darkness, death, animals or insects, etc.: all those phobias one hears about . . .

The Rite to the Dark Lady

Care must be taken to ensure all is prepared to satisfaction. You will need only one candle upon the Altar, and it should be either black, dark blue or dark green.

You will need incense of the Jasmine variety, called Night Queen, which is very strong and potent.

You will need your white Cord, Pentacle and Athame only.

It is advisable to have a piece of black cloth large enough to drape over your head at the 'work' point of the Ritual.

As usual wash with intent of purification, dry yourself and work your mixture of body oil well into your skin.

Wear nothing into your Circle that is not consecrated to your Art.

Light the Candle and Incense and close the Circle. Seat yourself before the Altar and go into meditation raising a humming chant to centre yourself.

When you are done, lift your Athame and invoke the Circle in the usual manner (see Esbat) and call the Guardians of the

Elements likewise.

Return to the Altar and raise the Pentacle above your head and say:

'**Dark Queen, Thou who dwelleth within the mouth of the Abyss, descend and show Thyself to me!**
I seek to be rid of all that dwells within the dark parts of my Soul!
I seek to bring all these things to light and therefore have naught between me and Thee!
I am confounded by the enemy of my Shadow self and would have Thee swallow it up and birth it as inspiration!'

Place the Pentacle upon the Altar and place the dark candle upon it.

Go into yourself by directing all your Will into the flame and begin to raise a Tantric chant, invoking the Goddess to aid you in your quest. When the Power is raised you are to visualise it as a Serpent wound around your thighs and genitals, lying passively and possessing the Power of the Dark Lady. *It is to remain there while you go on your Shadow voyage.*

Now take the black cloth and place it over your head.

Shrouded in darkness you are in the Cave of the Ancient Mother, the womb before Time.

Begin your Voyage by visualising a hole before you at the base of the Altar. Descend down this Tunnel and travel through it, observing all that you pass. If anything obstructs your passage you are to call upon the Power of the Serpent to deal with it on your behalf. When you reach the mouth of the Tunnel *take care to recall all that you see*. Let *nothing* slip your notice as you may make contact with a creature or being who will serve as an ally if you encounter problems.

You are to seek that which, to all appearances, is an aspect of yourself; also, that which appears to be you but which is not.

Voyage through this place until you encounter your Shadow. *Remember:* you are not to attack this Being, you are to *confront it* with the express purpose of using your knowledge to bring about an alliance. Call upon all tools of an Astral nature; call upon the Serpent. Most important is the summoning of your own *Magical Will*. The Shadow may incline to try to trick you into accepting your own fears as absolutes, but do not be fooled! Be aware, at all times, that this Shadow is your alter-ego and is therefore controlled by your conscious knowledge.

When your task is complete and the Shadow is submissive to your Will then call upon the Serpent to take the essences of fear and swallow them. They will be born at some later stage as creative inspiration.

When you are done then return the way you came, up through the Tunnel and back inside the Circle. Banish the hole and centre yourself.

Call again upon the Dark Lady to take back the Serpent of protection to Herself.

Then raise your Athame and say:

'**Thou art the Dark Sea from which all life comes and unto which all life returns! Marae, of the Dark Moon, I acknowledge the Three within the One and am humbled by Thy Might.**

Accept me as Thine own, daughter (son) of Darkness as well as of Light! I walk the Path mightily and shall not be seen lacking by men nor fates nor Gods!'

Remove the cloth from your head. Remove the candle from the Pentacle and make the sign of the Pentagram over the Candle saying:

'**As this Candle burns so shall my fears. When it dies so shall they cease to be!**'

Kiss the Pentacle saying:

'**The Great Mother is ever our refuge. I may enter the Circle with a heavy heart but with mirth do go forth and give my aid to the legions of the living!**'

First dismiss the Guardians of the Elements and banish the Circle, then put the still lighted Candle in a safe place where it is to be allowed to burn out.

Record the events of the night in your Grimoir.

Apart from a Rite of acknowledgement of the Dark Queen there is no need to perform the Voyage unless you find there is still more work to be done in that area.

The other purposes of the Dark Moon are there for you to discover for yourself. Always take great care to use the energy of this time sparingly and only in times of negative crisis when there is no other recourse, as the Power — if used incorrectly — will turn on the doer threefold.

SABBATS:
The Eightfold Wheel
of the Witch's Year

*Some notes to consider when meditating upon the deeper significance of
the Sabbats:*
1. The Rites to the Sun: the Solstices and Equinoxes.
2. The Rites to the Moon: the four Fire Festivals.

Winter Solstice: 22nd June (Sth Hemisphere);
                          22nd December (Nth Hemisphere)
                          Rebirth of the Sun God. The Boyhood
                          and Training of a King.

Spring Equinox: 22nd September (Sth Hemisphere);
                          21st March (Nth Hemisphere)
                          Symbolic and actual mating of the Sun
                          King with the Daughter of the Moon. His
                          Initiation as Priest King.

Summer Solstice: 22nd December (Sth Hemisphere);
                          22nd June (Nth Hemisphere)
                          Sacrifice of the Sun King. Death through
                          Reaping. Transformation of one Form
                          into another.

Autumn Equinox: 21st March (Sth Hemisphere);
                          22nd September (Nth Hemisphere)
                          Descent through the Underworld. Power
                          from the Dark Lord to the Maiden of
                          Initiation. (Descent of the Goddess as
                          Queen of the Underworld.)

Samhain:	1st May (Sth Hemisphere); 31st October (Nth Hemisphere)
	Dark Queen of the Labyrinth. Stone Goddess of the Serpents of Wisdom.
Feast of the Bride:	1st August (Sth Hemisphere); 2nd February (Nth Hemisphere)
	The Rise of the Child-Goddess. Virgin Queen. (Rite of puberty for females.) Honour of the Artemesian Way.
Beltaen:	31st October (Sth Hemisphere); 1st May (Nth Hemisphere)
	The Great Rite of the Goddess. Marriage to the Sun King through the Hunt. Festival of Spring.
Oimelc	2nd February (Sth Hemisphere); 1st August (Nth Hemisphere)
	Festival of the Goddess of Magic. The Time of the Enchantress. Rite of the High Priestess — Goddess Incarnate.

Sabbats

It is important to note that the impact of the Goddess is so great that She even affects a Witch's way of perceiving not only a Lunar Cycle but a daily and a seasonal one as well. A Witch's day goes from Sunset to Sunset and not Sunrise to Sunrise as is commonly accepted within our culture. The Night is not considered as the end of a day but as the womb of the new day, the birth of which occurs at sunrise. Mid-day is the full representation of the day and the time leading to sunset represents the onset of old age, wisdom, and the full-blown flower. As such Night is both Death and Rebirth and gives peace to seek into the deeper parts of our lives.

The Witch's Sabbats are divided into two groups: the Solstices and Equinoxes and the four Fire Festivals. The first group of four Sabbats are devoted to the God (therefore the male of the species and also the conscious intellect; all principles of Fire) and the second four are devoted to the Goddess (therefore to the female of the species and also the subconscious, intuitive nature).

The symbology of each Festival is to be considered for its personal implications; there are times both externally and internally in the cycles of existence for activity and passivity and to flow with the course of these times both personally and environmentally as well as spiritually is the true key to harmony. The enactment of Ritual is to acknowledge and participate in the Great Wheel of the Universe (as we know it), therefore allowing the externalisation of the deeper paths of personal passage.

Winter Solstice

For the Ritual you will need a brazier or an open fire. Gather woodchips, pine cones, dry kindling of pine. Acorns and leaves can adorn the Altar. You will need a red candle plus your four white candles to symbolise the four Elemental Gateways. You will need frankincense and cinnamon mix for your Incense plus a vial of musk or oakmoss oil, cakes and wine.

(This Ritual is written with the Female Witch in mind, so if you are male then read the following material and work without the use of the oils, using visualisation to assist you.)

The Ritual

Your Altar should face North.

Bathe with intent of purification.

Prepare all things, including the setting-up of the brazier or fireplace with woods in readiness for lighting.

Place upon the Altar your Athame, Wand, Pentacle, Cup, cakes, wine, oil, red candle and Incense.

There is no need to use the white Cord as a Circle boundary if you are working indoors; just place the four white candles at the compass points.

Light the four white candles and the Incense.

Seat yourself before the Altar and go into meditation raising a humming chant to centre yourself.

When you are ready then invoke the Circle in the usual manner and invoke the Elemental Guardians.

Seat yourself before the Altar and take the red candle.

Begin at its middle and rub the essential oil along it to its base, then go from the middle to the top until the candle is well oiled. Take it to the North Elemental Gate and light it from the candle there. Place it back upon the Altar.

Take your Athame in your left hand and the Wand in your right and raise both arms aloft and say:

'By Night's Dark Shade and in this Ritual Time
Most Ancient of the Gods on Thee I call!
Remembrance of past lives be awakened in me
And full knowledge of the Seed that I bear!
I claim my Life, my Freedom and my Light!
Part of all Light that flows eternally.
I am the Mirror of the Whole
Kindred of Star and Stone and Green Wood Tree.
Awaken in me the Power of Thy Will,
Kindle within me Thy Eternal Flame,
Accept me as Thine own, Priestess and Witch,
O, Power of Life that this Universe did frame!'

Kneel before the Altar, replace the Wand upon it.

Place the Cup filled with wine upon the Pentacle and form the sign of the Pentagram over it saying:

'Thou art the Cup of the Wine of Life and the Cauldron of Inspiration and the Womb of the Immortal Mother!'

Place your Athame blade within the Cup and say:

'The Cup is the Symbol of Woman and the Goddess. The Athame is the Symbol of Man and God; co-joined they are the blessed union that produces the three drops of Inspiration, the Creation Continuous!'

Sprinkle the consecrated wine over the cakes and with the middle finger of the Right Hand use the wine to draw the sign of the Pentagram upon your forehead. Raise the Cup and drink a little in honour of the Gods.

Take the oil in your left hand and your Athame in your right and draw the sign of the Pentagram over it saying:

'**Thou art the Essence of Blessing; whereupon Thou touchest all is blessed. Thou art the healing oil, the balm of the Initiate and the juices of the Sky Goddess! Mayest Thou aid me in all things Sacred!**'

So doing, stand and, placing a little oil on your finger, touch first both your feet saying:

'**Blessed be these feet made to walk the Path of the High Gods!**'

Touch both knees with oil saying:

'**Blessed be these knees made to kneel at the Altar of Infinity!**'

Touch the genitals with oil saying:

'**Blessed be this womb (phallus) without which no thing is born!**'

Touch the breasts with oil saying:

'**Blessed be these breasts (this breast) formed in beauty (strength)!**'

'Touch the lips with oil saying:

'**Blessed be these lips made only to speak the Sacred and Divine Names of the Lady and Lord of all Living!**'

Then take the red candle from the Altar and light the wood in the brazier or fireplace. Wait until it is well alight then drop three drops of oil into the fire.

If you are robed then disrobe, seat yourself before the fire and raise a chant of Power. When it is at its peak then stop, take the oil and rub it well into your belly whilst chanting the following:

'**One who has been!
One who is yet to be!
One now stands before Thee whose Soul is open to Thee!
Split asunder the Darkness and Illumine the Earth**

Both Within and Without!
Fill our Souls with Thy rebirth
That we may walk a little further,
Reach a little Higher,
That we may see the Far Horizon
With the eyes of the Eagle!
Complete the Ending that we may begin a new Spiral!
As the new is born so the old shall die
So that the old shall live in tomorrow's Sun.
Blessed be the Son!
Blessed be the Sun of Creation!'

Go through the visualisation of the sensation of birthing and project the raised energy of the chant at your own heart's centre and thence through your whole being.

Take the cakes and wine and eat and drink to the Sun God, then say:

'The Time of the Sun King Artu is the time of the Some becoming the One!
I call blessed the Light as I call blessed the Darkness!'

The Rite is ended of the Winter Solstice.

Allow the red candle to burn down.

Dismiss the Elemental Guardians and banish the Circle.

Any relevant information or impressions received during the Rite are to be recorded in your Grimoir.

Spring Equinox

For this Ritual you will need a freshly cut and stripped willow wand, blue dye (if using natural dye then see the end of this chapter for a list of plants available and directions for their preparation), a brazier or open fire, and a cauldron or fireproof vessel for the preparation of the dye. You will need your Athame, your usual Wand, Pentacle, Cup, a green candle for the Altar and four blue candles for the Elemental Gateways. You will also need wine and cakes, and essential oil of musk or oak moss. Your Incense will be of sandalwood and cedarwood. Have enough kindling and wood chips to have a goodly fire in your fireplace or brazier (pine is best), and your white Cord if working outdoors.

The Ritual
Bathe with intent of purification.

Prepare all things including the setting up of the brazier or fireplace with wood in readiness for lighting. Have the dye in the cauldron or fire-proof vessel.

Place upon the Altar the specially procured and stripped willow wand, your usual Wand, the Athame, Cup, Pentacle, wine, cakes, oil, green candle and Incense.

Place the blue candles at the compass points of the Elemental Gateways.

Light the four Elemental candles and the Incense.

Seat yourself before the Altar and go into meditation by raising a humming chant to centre yourself.

When ready, invoke the Circle in the usual manner and invoke the Guardians of the Elemental Gateways.

Seat yourself before the Altar and take the green candle.

Begin at the centre and rub the oil well into the candle from the centre to base then from centre to tip. Light it from the candle at the point of the North and place it back upon the Altar on top of the Pentacle.

Take your Athame in your left hand and the Wand in your right hand and raise them above you saying:

'By Night's Dark Shade and in this Ritual Time
Most Ancient of Gods on Thee I call!
Remembrance of past lives be awakened in me
And full knowledge of the Seed that I bear!
I claim my Life, my Freedom, my Light!
Part of all Light that flows eternally.
I am the mirror of the Whole
Kindred of Stár and Stone and Green Wood Tree.
Awaken in me the Power of Thy Will
Kindle within me Thy Eternal Flame,
Accept me as Thine own, Priestess (Priest) and Witch,

O, Power of Life that this Universe did frame!'

Kneel before the Altar, replace the Wand upon it. Fill the Cup with wine and, with your Athame, form the sign of the Pentagram over it saying:

'Thou art the Cup of the Wine of Life and the Cauldron of Inspiration and the Womb of the Immortal Mother!'

Place the blade of your Athame within the Cup and say:

'The Cup is the Symbol of Woman and the Goddess. The Athame is the Symbol of Man and God; co-joined they are the blessed union that produces the three drops of Inspiration, the Creation Continuous!'

Sprinkle the Consecrated Wine over the Cakes and, with the middle finger of the right hand use the Wine to draw the sign of the Pentagram upon your forehead. Raise the Cup and drink a little in honour of the Gods.

If you are using a new vial of oil then consecrate it now. Place a little of the oil on your finger, touch both feet with the oil saying:

'Blessed be these feet made to walk the Path of the High Gods!'

Touch both knees with oil saying:

'Blessed be these knees made to kneel at the Altar of Infinity!'

Touch the genitals saying:

'Blessed be this womb (phallus), without which no thing is born!'

Touch the breasts with oil saying:

'Blessed be these breasts (this breast) formed in beauty (strength)!'

Touch the lips saying:

'Blessed be these lips made only to speak the Sacred and Divine Names of the Lady and Lord of all Living!'

Then take the green candle and light the wood in the brazier or fireplace. Wait until it is well alight and place the vessel of dye within it till it is warm. Remove it when ready and place it at the foot of the Altar. Hold the Athame over it and bless it with the sign of the Pentagram. Add some of the consecrated oil then say:

'The coming together of the Sun Child at the time of manhood with the Priestess of the Moon is His Initiation into the Realm of High King. All upon the Earth is at one with this Divine Union, the fruit of Magic. The union of male and female is the glorification of the Island outside of Time. The Great Stag hunts the Great Stag and the Daughter of the Goddess calls the tune!'

Take the dye and draw the symbol of the Crescent Moon on your forehead (Priestess only) saying:

'I am the daughter of the Goddess. Through me She is seen amongst women and unto me all men must pay their due!'

Take the willow bough and dip it within the Cauldron until it is blue and say:

'The Rite of the Blessed Union will continue. No man will seek his Kingdom unless it be at the Will of the Goddess and no King shall reign without the gifts She gives. Evoe!!
Evoe!!
The Sungod is Thrice-Crowned Lord of the One!'

Lay the bough at the base of the Cup.

Raise a chant of Power and at the apex hold the Power steady. Go on a visionary voyage to the Island of the Sacred King. There you will see the Priestesses of the Moon all with the blue Crescent upon their brows. See the Priest of the Sun, painted with the blue dye and crowned with the horns of the King Stag take the Lady upon the Altar of His Initiation. The conception is the Child of Summer. Go with the vision until its natural ending then return and fulfil the chant.

Send the energy of the chant to the Higher Astral to add to the power of all others who work this Night for the good of the Earth.

When you are done take the cakes and wine and eat and drink in honour of the Thrice-Crowned King. Then say:

'The Seed that is sown in Spring will become the Flower of Harvest to all. As Nature flourishes so also do we.
The sword of Light has shown us His strength, the Great Mother has shown us Her Way.
Let us remember to be also beautiful for Her!
So Mote It Be!'
Leave the green candle to burn out.
The Rite is ended: farewell the Elemental Guardians and banish the circle.

Take the willow bough into your garden and bury it there. Pour the Consecrated Wine over the site in libation and scatter what is left of the Cakes to the birds.

To make the dye use one of the following:
Flowers of either cornflower or hollyhock
> *or*
root of elecampain
> *or*
the leafy branches of the indigo (powder available)
> *or*
the leaves of woad.

Soak (flowers or leaves) in rainwater overnight and boil next day for a minimum of 30 minutes; if using roots or leafy branches then soak 24 hours.

When 'cooked' leave to cool then strain through muslin and use the liquid!

Summer Solstice

For this Ritual you will need to gather as many different grains as you can, a mortar and pestle to grind them, and a brazier on which to burn them. Do not use the fireplace unless it is cleared of all past ashes. Gather wood chips and a small quantity of pine kindling. Have for your Altar the usual Ritual tools, yellow candle, Incense or myrrh and olibanum, wine and cakes, essential oil from previous Equinox, and four white candles for the Elemental Gateways.

The Ritual

Bathe with intent of purification. Oil your body.

Prepare all things including the setting up of the brazier with wood in readiness for lighting.

Place all Ritual objects upon the Altar and the point candles at the Elemental Gateways.

Light the four Elemental candles and the Incense.

Close the Circle if using the white Cord outdoors.

Seat yourself and go into meditation raising a humming chant to centre yourself.

When you are ready, invoke the Guardians of the Elements.

Seat yourself before the Altar and take the yellow candle and rub the essential oil into it beginning at the centre and working it to the base then from centre to top. Light it from the candle at the North Gateway and replace it upon the Altar.

Place the grains within the mortar and grind them down.

Take your Athame in your left hand and the Wand in your right and raise them above you saying:

'By Night's Dark Shade and in this Ritual Time
Most Ancient of Gods on Thee I call!
Remembrance of past lives be awakened in me
And full knowledge of the Seed that I bear!
I claim my Life, my Freedom, my Light!
Part of all Light that flows eternally.
I am the mirror of the Whole
Kindred of Star and Stone and Green Wood Tree.
Awaken within me the Power of Thy Will,
Kindle within me Thy Eternal Flame,
Accept me as Thine own, Priestess and Witch,
O, Power of Life that this Cosmos did Frame!'

Kneel before the Altar and replace the Wand upon it. Pour wine into the Cup and with your Athame form the sign of the Pentagram over it saying:

'Thou art the Cup of the Wine of Life
And the Cauldron of Inspiration and the Womb of the

Immortal Mother!'

Place the blade of your Athame within the Cup and say:

'The Cup is the Symbol of Woman and the Goddess. The Athame is the Symbol of Man and God; co-joined they are the blessed union that produces the three drops of Inspiration, the Creation Continuous!'

Sprinkle the Consecrated Wine over the Cakes and, with the middle finger of the right hand, use the Wine to draw the sign of the Pentagram upon your forehead. Raise the Cup and drink a little in honour of the Gods.

Take the oil, place a little of it on your finger, and touch both your feet saying:

'Blessed be these feet made to walk the Path of the High Gods!'

Touch both knees saying:

'Blessed be these knees made to kneel at the Altar of Infinity!'

Touch the genitals with oil saying:

'Blessed be this womb (phallus) without which no thing is born!'

'Touch the breast saying:

'Blessed be these breasts (breast) formed in beauty (strength)!'

Touch the lips saying:

'Blessed be these lips made only to speak the Sacred and Divine Names of the Lady and Lord of all Living!'

Then take the yellow candle and light the brazier with it. Keep the wood packed closely. Pour a little of the oil onto it, then add the crushed grains.

Raise a chant of Power and when it reaches the apex hold it. Raise your Athame aloft and say:

'Great One!
Great King of the Sun, Lord of the Flame!
Power of the Light I invoke Thee in Thy most Ancient and Sacred Names; Artu! Llugh! Cernunnos! Midrael! Balin! Herne!

Thou dost Reign Supreme within Thy Lands!
Raise up Thy Sword of the Ancient Pact!
Put to flight the powers of dark ignorance of Thy Ways!
Give us fair woodlands and green fields, blossoming orchards and ripening fruits.
Bring us to stand upon the Hill of Vision and show to us the Realms of the Gods!'

Take the Pentagram and hold it to the brazier saying:
'The Body of the King is as ashes upon the field.
The Four Winds lift the Will of the Mighty One and scatter it to the Faraway.
The Sun is the Glory and the Lover of the Lady.
Yet remember the Time of Decline.
Fear not the Death for the Womb of the Mother is also the Reaper and all that Becomes is through Her Higher Change.
Remember now that the Goddess will raise the God and Her Lover shall be Her Son as He Spirals the Greater Journey!'

Place the Pentacle upon the Altar and go into your Vision. See the King Thrice Crowned upon the Throne of the One Land.

He is Dying.

With Him is the High Priestess of the Isle of the Moon Goddess And the High Bard of the King, the One Land and the Isle of the Priestesses of the Moon.

She is there to take from Him the Sword of His Right to Reign; To take its power back from whence it came until He reigns again. The High Bard is there to listen and recall all that takes place so that His Name is not forgotten in the Darkness of His Night. Attending the High Priestess are the youngest of the Isle and the Ancient Woman, wise in the ways of the Night and the Passage.

Observe all that takes place.

The Seeds of Summer are burned in Sacrifice to the Sun God and the Chant of Power is raised with the smoke by the

Priestesses of the Moon so that the Passage of the Sun King, Child of the Sun and Moon, shall be in Truth and Wisdom.

When the Vision has faded then complete the raising of your own chant and direct it to the smoke of your Fire. Merge your own wishes with the smoke for the future.

Now plunge the Wand into the Wine and say:

'**The Spear to the Cauldron, the Lance to the Grail, Spirit to Flesh, Man to Woman, Sun to Earth!**'

The Rite is ended.

Allow the Altar Candle to burn down.

Dismiss the Elemental Guardians and banish the Circle. Spread the ashes of the brazier over your garden as compost.

Autumn Equinox

For this Ritual you will need two Altar candles, one black and one gold. No point candles are used for the Elemental Gateways. You will need your black headcloth and a gift of silver for the Earth. Take matches into the Circle.

Have the usual Ritual tools on the Altar, and also Incense of musk. You do not use the brazier for this Sabbat.

The Ritual

Bathe with intent of purification. Oil your body. Wear no jewellery into the Circle and, if possible, you are to work skyclad.

Place all things upon the Altar including the gift of silver, and the black and the gold candles.

Light the Incense.

Close your Circle with the white Cord if working outdoors.

Seat yourself before the Altar and go into meditation using the soft humming chant to centre yourself.

When you are ready then invoke the Circle in the usual manner and invoke the Elemental Guardians.

Take the matches and light the black candle saying:

'**In the Name of the Ancient Gods of my Chosen Way,**

and under their protection, this Rite now begins!'

Using the black candle light the gold candle and stand them side by side upon the Altar.

Now take up the Wand and rub it with oil saying:

'The God of Light now dwells within the Labyrinth of Darkness.
He dwells enthroned, Judge of Gods and Men, High Leader of the Hosts of Shades.
Yet even as He dwells within the Temple of Death
So dwelleth He within the Secret Seed;
Seed of the Grain, Seed of the Flesh, Hidden of the Earth,
Seed of the Stars, the Crystal Seed of the Fire.
In Him is Life and Life is the Light of Man,
That which was never born and therefore cannot die . . .
The Wise weep not!'

Take your Athame and make the sign of the Pentagram over the black candle saying:

'The House of Death is also the House of Birth, The Ancient Way, the Temple of Initiation!'

Then make the sign of the Pentagram over the gold candle saying:

'Darkness comes before Light but always does Light follow
Darkness, the One becoming the Other in the Great Wheel!'

Replace your Athame upon the Altar and take up the oil and placing a little of it on your finger touch both feet saying:

'Blessed be these feet made to walk the Path of the High Gods!'

Touch both knees saying:

'Blessed be these knees made to kneel at the Altar of Infinity!'

Touch the breast saying:

'Blessed be these breasts (this breast) formed in beauty (Strength)!'

Touch both the lips saying:

'Blessed be these lips made only to speak the Sacred and Divine Names of the Lady and Lord of all Living!'

Then stand with the Athame in your right hand, raise your arms and say:

'By Night's Dark Shade in this Ritual Time
Most Ancient of Gods on Thee I call!
Remembrance of past lives be awakened in me
And the full knowledge of the Seed that I bear!
I claim my Life, my Freedom, my Light!
Part of all Light that flows eternally.
I am the Mirror of the Whole
Kindred of Star and Stone and Green Wood Tree.
Awaken within me the Power of Thy Will,
Kindle within me Thy Eternal Flame,
Accept me as Thine own, Priestess and Witch,
O, Power of Life that this Universe did frame!'

Now make the sign of the Pentagram over the gift of silver with your Athame. Take it in your hands, place the black cloth over your head.

Raise a chant of Power and at its apex hold it and begin your Vision:

You are standing upon a vast, empty plain. The only thing that you can see is a cairn of standing stones. Walk to the centre of these stones and call upon the mighty Warrior Goddess of the Moon and the Ancient One of the Fates to be with you on your descent into the Labyrinth of the Dark King.

A shaft of Moonlight reaches out and strikes the silver within your hands and it forms a talisman of Lunar Force shedding Light upon the stone steps at your feet.

You begin your descent into the Labyrinth. The Way is narrow and black save for the Moon Talisman. You wend your way down for many miles right into the belly of the Earth Mother. The passageway winds and turns in upon itself but always the Talisman glows brighter if you appear to go the wrong way.

Eventually you enter into a vast cavern lit by the phos-
phorescence upon the walls of the place of the Dark King. You
see Him ahead, seated upon a Throne made from the same
Stone of the Cavern. You were fearful of how He would appear
in this place of Death but He is Magnificent, a Monarch of
absolute Glory. Beside Him is a Throne of Obsidian and
seated upon it is a Queen. She is Veiled, and wearing a Crown
that is the same shape as the Moon Talisman you hold. The
King beckons you. You go and stand before Him and He
says:

'You come to this Place naked yet you carry with you the Gift
of the Light of the High Queen. I shall not hold you here as I
shall not be held!'

You pass to the Queen. She raises Her Veil and all that you
can see are birds, soft rain, green fields, flowers, mountains
and rivers — all things of Earth. She laughs, and it is the sound
of the wind amongst the trees. You laugh also and you hear, as
though from the very walls of the Place:

'I am the Beauty of the Green Earth and the White Moon
among the Stars and the Mystery of the Waters and the Desire
of the heart of Man.

'Call unto My Soul, arise and come unto Me; for I am the
Soul of Nature who giveth joy to the Universe, from Me all
things proceed and unto Me all things must return! So before
My Face, the beloved of Gods and men, let thine innermost,
divine self be unfolded in the Rapture of the Infinite. Let My
worship be within the heart that rejoiceth, for behold, all acts
of love and pleasure are my Rituals! Therefore let there be
compassion, honour and humility, mirth and reverence
within you. And if thou thinkest to seek for Me know that thy
seeking and yearning will avail thee not unless thou knowest
the Mystery . . . that if that which thou seekest thou findest not
within thee thou wilt never find it without! For behold! I have
been with thee from the beginning and I am that which is
attained at the end of all desire!'

You bow, walk back to the High King, bow and leave the way

you came to dwell upon that which you have seen.

Return to the Circle and place the silver upon the Altar. Remove the black cloth. Snuff the black candle. Stand and dismiss the Guardians of the Elements and banish the Circle.

Keep the Talisman safely for yourself.

Allow the gold candle to burn down.

The Rite is done.

Samhain

This is the end of the old year and the beginning of the new. It signifies the time of the Crone and Death; the time when the barrier between the worlds is at its finest, the dark, silent time at the onset of Winter.

It is significant to note that the colder months are considered as times of personal 'hibernation' where much study and introspection are done in preparation for the new Cycle.

Samhain (pronounced *Seveen*) is considered the time when the bridge between the seen and the unseen is most accessible and therefore much of this night is devoted to scrying and contact with dimensions other than the physical.

The Ritual

For this Rite you will need a loaf of home-made bread, a cauldron prepared with dry leaves, twigs and sweet-smelling herbs, a mirror for scrying, your black head cloth plus all Ritual equipment. Use your white Cord for protection whether inside or outside and use four white candles for the Elemental Gateways plus a red and a white one for your Altar.

You will also require your red or green Cord for this night. Set up your Altar and prepare the 'working' area. Bathe with intent of purification and oil your body. Close your Circle after lighting Incense and the Elemental candles.

Seat yourself before the Altar and go into meditation raising a soft humming chant to centre yourself.

Cast your Circle, invoking the Goddess and the God to bear witness and to protect your work on this Night.

Invoke the Elemental Guardians as usual.

Light the white Altar candle from the South Gateway and light the red one from it.

Pour red wine into your Cup and raise it aloft saying:

'**Mighty Mother, Dark Queen, bless this wine, may it be as the Cauldron of Inspiration which contains three drops of Wisdom for the World.**'

Hold the Cup over the symbolic Elements on your Altar and say:

'**Creatures of Fire, Creatures of Air, Creatures of Earth, Creatures of Water, friends in Life, friends in Death, gather Ye here in the Dark Queen's Name, as She gathers Earth to Her again!**'

Stand and walk around the Circle holding the Wine aloft then return to the Altar, raise the Cup in honour of the Lady and drink. Then say:

'**Hail! The Queen, Dark Queen! Mother of Tide and Change!**'

Take the essential oil and make the sign of the Pentagram upon your forehead, then rub the mirror with it saying:

'**I Charge this object with Life for this Night only. May it show that which I seek to See!**'

Sit with the Mirror in your lap and begin humming to raise a chant of Power. Centre all of the forces of your chant into a beam that extends from the Mirror to your forehead to the apex of your Circle. When it is secure, say:

'**Come ye of the Ancient Way! Come ye of the Sacred Isle!**

Hear now the voice of my inner longing! For I call upon those of the Ancient Wisdom!

Back through the Gates of Time to the Time of all Knowledge!'

Light the Cauldron with the red candle, wait until it is

ablaze, add Incense and sweet herbs then say:

'I have lit the beacon; be ye guided to this Place, made Sacred to the Goddess of my Art!

Hear me, all those who would be of my house! The gulf between the Worlds exists not this Night. Approach all those who are of the Ancient Wisdom!

Come to be with me all those who Will of the Art!

The Cup is filled in the Name of the Three, for I would see and speak with thee and I would see that which is yet to be.

Great Goddess grant Insight and Serenity.

Let the Light of Love guard the sleep of the child.

O Lady of the Unborn cast back Thy cloak

And grant to me the sight!'

Now focus on the Mirror and concentrate on what appears there whilst listening for the voices of the Ancient Wisdom.

When you are done, sprinkle the bread with Wine. Take a portion and eat and drink in the Goddess's Name. Keep the remainder which is to be shared with those people about you for whom you care. Remember to say nothing of its origins but say only that it is food shared as a loving exchange.

When you are done, say:

'Ye are my Sisters and my Brothers of the Past, Present and Future. May we walk upon the Silver Path throughout Time through all the Times that are yet to be. We have met this Night and remembered. We have Known this Night. Time is no time, barriers are naught but Illusion. All Life is Endless!

I bid thee go now, all called here, disturbing not those who would fear thee, nor harming any substance of this Earth.

Remember me, for we are One, for the Gods have seen and it is They who call the Tune!

So Mote It Be!'

Raise your Athame high and say:

'All that is not for my highest good is now past as is the

year that is no more. Might that I seek knowledge from that which has been and seek, within the New Year, the Wisdom to be that which the Mighty Mother sees fit that I be! Blessed Be the Ancient Woman!'

Farewell the Guardians of the Elemental Gateways and banish the Circle. Leave the Altar candles to burn down. Record all that you saw, in your Grimoir.

Give a small portion of the bread and the consecrated Wine to the Earth in libation and, in the days following, share the bread with those you love.

The Rite is ended.

Feast of the Bride

This Ritual celebrates the Birth of the Goddess through the female of the species. The feminine principle of inner power is manifest at the time of this Rite.

This is also the time of the Child-Goddess or Virgin Queen, and symbolic of the Rite of the Neophyte where the Priestess or Priest makes definite and certain moves to walk the Path of the true Initiate.

Honour of the Artemesian Way is to be considered as the Vision of this Ritual. The Freedom of the Wild and the glorification of the Ancient and Primitive Force represent the Power that is invoked in all workings. Here we see the Power in its essential, pre-intellectual aspects — the anarchistic, wild, time of the 'unpossessed' woman.

The Ritual

For this Rite you will need a specially prepared essential oil consisting of a mixture of rose, pennyroyal and jasmine. Add a little of this mixture to pure olive oil. Have this ready for the Ritual. You will also need red wine and flower seeds of the strongly scented variety, and Incense of rose and jasmine.

Have all your usual tools upon the Altar plus a pink candle.

Bathe with intent of purification and dry yourself but do not oil your body at this time.

Place the Gateway candles at each point and light them.

Light the Incense.

Light the Altar candle from the one located in the South.

Seat yourself before the Altar and go into meditation, raising a soft humming chant to centre yourself.

Take the essential oil mix and place a little on your fingers and touch both feet saying:

'**Blessed be these feet made to walk the Path of the High Gods!**'

Touch both knees with oil saying:

'**Blessed be these knees made to kneel at the Altar of Infinity!**'

Touch the genitals saying:

'**Blessed be this womb (phallus) without which no thing is born!**'

Touch the breast with oil saying:

'**Blessed be these breasts (this breast) formed in beauty (strength)!**'

Touch the lips saying:

'**Blessed be these lips made only to speak the Names of the Lady and Lord of all Living!**'

Form the sign of the Pentagram over the wine saying:

'**The Cup is the symbol of Woman and the Goddess! The Athame is the symbol of Man and God!**'

Place the blade into the Cup saying:

'**They are the Blessed Union that produces the Three Drops of Inspiration, the Creation Continuous!**'

Make the sign of the Pentagram on your own forehead with the wine.

Stand and spread your arms and legs to form the sign of the Pentagram with your body and invoke:

'**Five are the Points of Fellowship. Here where Lance and Grail unite! And feet and knees and breast and lip! Here the Gate of the Universe wherein all things abound**

For the Glory of the Spiral Dance of the Cosmos.
Thou who art Eternal Queen with horn of Moon Thrice
Crowned,
See here the Child of the Star-born!
We are One with Thee, Thou art One with us!'
     Kneel and raise your Athame high saying:
     'Thee, I invoke, Wild Woman, Virgin Queen of the
Mountain and of the Sea! Wind of the Desert and Rain of
the deepest untouched Forest! Be here and form within me,
Thy Priestess, the Knowledge of your boundless Freedom.
Let naught possess my Soul for I am One with Thee; Virgin
born I pledge my Path to the Whole that is the Thrice
Crowned Mistress of the Moon!'
     Replace your Athame upon the Altar and take the Cup.
Hold it over the symbols of the Four Elements saying:
     'Blessed by Fire, the Cup of the Wine of Life!
Blessed by Air, the Cup of the Wine of Life!
Blessed by Earth, the Cup of the Wine of Life!
Blessed by Water, the Cup of the Wine of Life!'
     Then raise the Cup and drink *all* the contents.
     Raise a chant of Power and at the apex hold and go into your
Vision.
     In front of the Altar is a Tunnel. Enter and travel until you
exit into a cave. There you will see a gathering of thirteen
Priestesses standing before the statue of the Virgin Queen. You
join them. Your Initiation into the ranks of the Children of the
Wild Goddess is to take place upon this Night. You disrobe
and they oil your body with the consecrated oil that has been
specially prepared for the Rite. You kneel at the Altar upon
which is only the bowl of seeds. You raise the seeds and invoke
the Lady to be with you. Replace the seeds upon the Altar. You
feel the presence of the Queen enter into you as the process of
defloration takes place at the hands of the High Priestess of
this Sacred Place, Womb of the Ancient Mother.
     You then stand and shed your Virgin-blood upon the seeds
which shall be grown within the confines of the Wild Places in

honour of your Initiation into Womanhood where they will grow, uncut and untouched, and be allowed to go their own way without cultivation.

You kiss each Priestess in turn and give thanks this Night to the Holy Goddess.

Then return up the tunnel to your own Sacred Circle. Kneel and say:

'There are Candles still to burn,
I am here to burn them!
There are secrets to be learned,
I am here to learn them!
As long as the Moon shall rise
And the Stars shall turn!
Beyond illusion and lies
I cease not to learn.
Beyond the Doorway of Time
And out into the Night
In search of Mystery
And the wonder of Light!'

Then stand and say in conclusion:

'Great Goddess let your servants be many and secret.
Let them rule the many and the known
For man is ever a Star and woman a Moon;
To him is the secret of the Winged Flame
To her the secret of the Starlight.
I may enter the Circle with a heavy heart
With mirth I go forth and with thanksgiving
Do pleasure on Earth
And give my aid to the legions of the living!'

Before you end rub the Consecrated oil all over your body, missing no part, as this is also the Rite of Naming and should you seek to take a Sacred Name it may be given during your sleep state on this Night and it is best to be properly prepared.

When you are done then farewell the Guardians of the Elemental Gateways and banish the Circle.

Plant the seeds in some inaccessible place where they are to be allowed to grow unhindered by anyone!

Beltaen

This is the Rite of the Goddess in Her aspect as Mother of all Living. As such it is considered Her time of Greatest Beauty. This Rite is the usual period for Handfastings to be held. (A Handfasting is a Witch's form of marriage; it does not 'bind' one person to the other, as this practice of possession does not exist in Witchcraft, but instead is a pledge of loving between two people for the Passage of a year and a day, or from then for as long as love lasts.)

It is the time of the melding of forces between the male and the female in Force as well as Form — the Festival of Spring.

The Ritual

Where there is abundance, the picking of flowers to adorn your Altar and Circle is permissable. You will use oil and incense of rose and lavender — the Incense mixed with orris root.

Bake a sweet cake using honey as the main ingredient. Use red wine for the Rite and have all usual Ritual tools upon the Altar.

Bathe with intent of purification and lavishly rub your body with prepared oil.

Have also a green candle for the Altar.

Prepare the Circle as usual. Light the four Gateway candles and the Incense.

Seat yourself and go into meditation raising a soft humming chant to centre yourself. Then raise your Athame and say:

'In Temples of Stones, Herbs and Flowers
The Ancient Truth is ours.
Mysteries in the heart burning strong
We ne'er will forsake the Earthlove Song,
O Mighty Mother

Blessed be Thy Name!'

Cast the Circle in the usual manner and invoke the Guardians of the Elemental Gateways to be with you on this Night. Take your Athame and form the sign of the Pentagram over the wine and pour it into the Cup. Put the blade of your Athame into the Cup and say:

'The Cup is the symbol of Woman and the Goddess. The Athame is the symbol of Man and God! They are the blessed union that produces the three drops of Inspiration, the Creation Continuous!'

Stand with arms and legs forming the sign of the Pentagram and say:

'Five are the points of fellowship. Here where Lance and Grail unite! And feet and knees and breast and lip!
Here the Gate of the Universe wherein all things abound
For the glory of the Spiral Dance of the Cosmos.
Thou who art Eternal Queen with Horn of Moon Thrice Crowned,
See here the Child of the Star-born!
We are One with Thee, Thou art One with us!'

Take the essential oil and make the sign of the Pentagram over it with your Athame.

Touch both feet with oil saying:

'Blessed be these feet made to walk the Path of the High Gods!'

Touch both knees with the oil saying:

"Blessed be these knees made to kneel at the Altar of Infinity!'

Touch the genitals with oil saying:

'Blessed be this womb (phallus) without which no thing is born!'

Touch the breast saying:

'Blessed be these breasts (this breast) formed in beauty (strength)!'

Touch the lips saying:

'Blessed be these lips made only to speak the Sacred and

Divine Names of the Lady and Lord of all Living!'

Then kneel and say:

'She is the beauty of the Green Earth and the White Moon among the Stars and the Mystery of the Waters and the Desire of the heart of Man.

Call unto Her Soul, arise and come, for She is the soul of Nature Who giveth joy to the Universe.

From Her all things proceed and unto Her all things must return.

Before Her face, beloved of Gods and men, let thine innermost divine self be unfolded in the rapture of the Infinite.

Let Her worship be within the heart that rejoiceth, for Behold, all acts of Love and pleasure are Her Rituals.

Therefore let there be compassion, honour and humility, Mirth and reverence within.

And thou who thinkest to seek for Her know that thy seeking

And yearning will avail thee not unless thou knowest the Mystery,

That if that which thou seekest thou findest not within thee

Thou wilt never find it without for behold!

She hast been with thee from the beginning and She is that

Which is attained at the end of all desire!'

Now set yourself before the Altar and raise a chant of Power. At its apex go within your Vision.

See the Sacred Isle. Apple trees in blossom, every conceivable flower and tree in blossom. See a bower of grape leaves with the petals of roses covering the ground beneath it. The Lady is there; primally and gloriously beautiful, surrounded by the Priestesses of Her Way. Go and join them.

The Lady is big with Child. She is in labour and the Priestesses attend Her as She moans with the Power of the Ebb and Flow of the Birthing. Watch and glory as She bears down, legs in a squat.

Her hair is wild and flowing over Her breasts and belly. She is sweating and laughing and grunting and panting and loving every contraction that flows over Her.

Now the Head is crowning; the hair upon the Infant's head is as golden as the rising Sun. She lays back to enable the women to assist Her and share in the Birthing. She bears down and, with a shout of triumph, pushes out the Boychild. The Priestesses raise the Child to the Lady's belly where He lies until the Cord stops pulsing. The High Priestess then cuts the Cord and the Goddess lifts the Child to suckle at Her breast. She says:

'The Child was once my Lover and was once my Father and it shall be so again and again and again until the end of the Infinite!'

The Priestesses then deliver the placenta which is to be buried and another tree planted in that Place to blossom in another year.

You stay and share the joy that is part of all Life before you return to the Circle.

Lift the Cup and drink in honour of the Mother in all things.

Then you light the green candle in honour of the Night and leave it to burn down.

Sprinkle wine on the cakes and eat, remembering to keep some for libation.

Farewell the Guardians of the Elemental Gateways and banish the Circle.

The Rite is ended.

Oimelc

This is the Ritual of the Greater Magic of the Goddess, the Rite of the Sacred Enchantress and the Secret Sorceress.

It is the Rite of Honour of the High Priestess — the Goddess Incarnate. The highest aspirations of women are represented on this Night.

This is sometimes called the Feast of Faery, celebrating the

Hidden Children of the Goddess, those beings who exist in the Half-World outside of Time, the Sidhe. The God of Light, sometimes called Llugh, pays homage to the Goddess; He is as the Spear as She is as the Grail and reflection upon the tradition of Nimue and the Merlin would be of benefit when considering the significance of this Rite.

The Ritual
Prepare beforehand a bowl of water into which you are to add some blue dye; this is to act as a channel for your own invocations to the Mistress and provide a pool whereby you may see your own Magical, Archetypal image reflected in the Eye of the Goddess. Have with you your green or red Cord, red wine, a silver candle for the Altar, four blue candles for the Elemental Gateways, all tools Sacred to the Craft, essential oil and Incense of musk, jasmine and olibanum. You will need to use your white Cord as a boundary whether working indoors or out.

This is to be considered as one of the greatest celebratory Rites of the Goddess outside of the Esbat.

Bathe with intent of purification and oil your body well.

Light the Incense and the four Elemental candles and close the Circle. Seat yourself before the Altar and go into meditation raising a soft humming chant to centre yourself.

Stand and invoke the Circle and summon the Guardians of the Elements. Return to the Altar and take up the silver candle and, starting in the middle, rub with oil to its base concentrating on the act of consecration of your actions to the Will of the Goddess, then work from middle to top. This being done, light the Altar candle from the South and place it upon the Altar on the Pentacle.

Take your Athame and dip the blade into the Cup of wine saying:

'The Cup is the symbol of Woman and the Goddess. The Athame is the symbol of Man and God! They are the blessed union that produces the three drops of Inspiration, the Creation Continuous!'

Stand with your arms and legs forming the sign of the
Pentagram with your body and say:

'Five are the points of fellowship. Here where Lance and
Grail unite! And feet and knees and breast and lip!
Here the Gate of the Universe wherein all things abound
For the glory of the Spiral Dance of the Cosmos.
Thou who art Eternal Queen with Horn of Moon Thrice-
Crowned,
See here the Child of the Star-born!
We are One with Thee, Thou art One with us!'

Then take the essential oil and touch first both your feet
saying:

'Blessed be these feet made to walk the Path of the High
Gods!'

Then touch the knees with oil saying:

'Blessed be these knees made to kneel at the Altar of
Infinity!'

Then touch the genitals with oil saying:

'Blessed be this womb (phallus) without which no thing
is born!'

Touch the breast with oil saying:

'Blessed be these breasts (this breast) formed in beauty
(strength)!'

Touch the lips saying:

'Blessed be these lips made only to speak the Sacred and
Divine Names of the Lady and Lord of all Living!'

Then kneel and raise the Wand saying:

'By the Flame that burneth bright,
O Horned One!
I call Thy Name into the Night
O Ancient One!
Thee I invoke by the Moonled Sea
By the Standing Stone and the Twisted Tree.
By Moonlit meadow, on dusky Hill
When the haunted Tor is hushed and still;

Come to the Charm of the Chanted prayer
As the Moon bewitches the Midnight Air!
I evoke Thy Powers that potent bide
In shining stream and Secret Tide,
In Fiery Flame by Starlight pale,
In shadowy hosts that ride the gale,
By the ferndrakes, Faery haunted,
Of forests wild and woods Enchanted.
I speak the Spell your Power unlocks
Great Master of Solstice and Equinox!'
    Then lift your Athame as well and say:
    'I invoke Thee, Master of Magic!
Midrael! Artu! Llugh! Herne!
I call to Thee in the Names of the High Goddess!
I call upon your Sword of Light!
Summon for me the Queen of all Magic!
Call to Her to be with me here!
I am the Mirror of the Whole!
This is the Night of High Magic's Queen and I would see
That which is mine to See!'
    Then seat yourself before the Altar and form the sign of the Pentagram over the bowl of blue water.
Centre yourself and raise a Cone of Power using the Words 'IO-EVO-HE!'.
    At the apex of the Chant hold the Power within yourself and say:
    'O Lady of the Moon, Enchantment's Queen of Midnight, The Potent Sorceress,
O Lady from the Darkest Circle of Time,
Tailltiu! Tanith! Morgana! Dana! Cerridwen!
Artemis! Arianrhod! Diana! Hecate!
Your Power I invoke to aid me!
Your Moon, a Magic Mirror, rides the Sky,
Reflecting Mystic Light upon the Earth,
And every Moon your Threefold Image shines!

Mistress of Magic, Ruler of the Tides both seen and
unseen
Spinner of the Threads of Birth and Death and Fate,
Vast and Shadowed, to deepest Realms unseen,
Your Power I invoke to aid me!
O Lady of the Silver Light that shines in Magic Rays
Through deepest woodland glade and over Sacred and
Enchanted Hills,
At still of Night when Witches cast their Spells
When Spirit walks and strange Beings are abroad,
By the Dark Cauldron of your Inspiration,
Goddess Threefold upon Thee I call.
Your Power I invoke to aid me!
Your Power I invoke to aid me!
Your Power I invoke within this Circle NOW!'

Go back into chant and continue to build the Cone until
you are completely absorbed by it within your Sacred Space
then look deeply into the bowl of water and remember all that
you see. This is your Vision and it is to be unhindered by any
preconceived words. Take your time. When you are done keep
all invoked force that is within you but project the rest of the
Cone out through the apex of your Circle to be kept as a Star
within your Astral Temple for use in times of personal or
environmental need.

When you are centred again then say:

'Great Goddess, let your Servants be many and secret.
Let them rule the many and the known.
For Man is ever a Star and Woman a Moon.
To him is the secret of the Winged Flame,
To Her the secret of the Star Light.
We will rejoice in existence.
All sorrow is but Shadow that passes and is done
And always Life remains.
The Truth is the help and the hope of our Spells,
For it is understood that our Gods are of peace, joy and
laughter;

But they are also of vengeance to those who would direct evil
And evil will be treated in like manner by Them.
So fear not at all; neither men nor Fates nor Gods nor anything,
Not any power in heaven or earth.
The Great Mother is ever our refuge!
I may enter the Circle with a heavy heart
But with mirth do go forth
And with thanksgiving do pleasure on Earth
And give my aid to the legions of the living!'
   Raise your Cup and down the contents and say:
   '**So Mote It Be!**'
   Snuff the Silver Candle and keep it put away for any important work that you will do in the future.
   Send the Elemental Guardians back to their Realms and banish the Circle.
   The Rite is ended.

A Self-Initiation
There is an expression that 'Only a Witch can make a Witch' and this implies Initiation; even an hereditary-born needs to make that final commitment before being truly considered Witch/Priestess (Priest).
   If you find that you have tested what you feel, and that what you feel is the most certain thing in your life, then if Witch is what you feel then Witch is what you will become.
   Witchcraft implies commitment. If you are determined to progress alone then this Ritual will give you the guidelines to self-initiation. Remember 'As above, so below' — the knowledge of your certainty by the Forces beyond the physical. No Initiation can take place unless it is a two-fold one. If you have been approved by the Gods then physical Initiation will follow, given Time; if you are not being totally sincere in your desire to represent the Gods then all you will feel is hollow, false when working in the physical.

Initiation is not for everyone. A Pagan can follow the Rituals within these pages and gain satisfaction in what they do and never feel the desire to commit themselves further.

Failing to find a suitable Coven into which to be Initiated, you must seek affirmation as a Solitary.

The first step is to take a full Lunar Cycle to seek your Name. A Witch's Initiation Name is both Secret and Sacred; it contains all the essences of your own Power and is *never* spoken of unless it be to another Initiate for whom you have absolute trust and respect. You may be given your Name during periods of Ritual, Vision, Meditation or simply as Inspiration, knowing just what your Secret and Sacred Name is. However it will always be appropriate to your chosen Path and symbolic to that Path in some way.

The Ritual

It is required that you enter into a personal Initiation as seriously as if you were being Initiated at the discretion of a Witch already trained to the rank of High Priestess or High Priest. Therefore, you will be required to fast from Sunset of the day prior to your Self-Initiation and to speak as little as possible and then only when spoken to by those around you who have no knowledge of what you are doing. If you are lucky enough to have the support of a loved one then tell them of the preparation you are undertaking and have them assist you by giving you your silence and your space.

Spend those entire last hours in consideration of your chosen Path and be very certain that you are prepared to commit yourself to the Gods.

Three hours prior to the time that you have decided upon for the Rite set up your Circle in readiness.

Have within your Circle salt and water in separate containers, wine and Cup, Athame, Pentacle, Wand, White-hilted Knife (Boline), your red or green Cord, Thurible, Incense of frankincense and myrrh with a sandalwood base. Have prepared oil for your body and have it within the Circle.

Have four white candles for the Elemental Gateways — three silver, one gold and one white for the Altar.

Now, for this Night you will have made or procured, without haggling over price, a silver Pentagram; it were best if it could be made by your own hand but this is not always possible. Find a jeweller who will make it to your specifications (an example is shown here):

There are many amulets worn by Witches to their own specifications but the Pentagram is a universal symbol acknowledged by all occultists the world over.

Have this amulet on the Altar ready for the Ritual — it is your gift of Initiation to yourself and also the symbol of your own commitment. It should be worn constantly from this time forward.

Bathe with intent of purification.

Remember to take matches to the Circle with you.

Enter the Circle naked and without any jewellery; let nothing hold up your hair and wear no makeup, aftershave, perfume or deodorant. You are symbolically about to die as the person that you once were and to be reborn as Priestess or Priest of your Art, and you must enter the Circle as an unborn creature.

Cast your Circle but do not invoke the Elemental Guardians. Light only the white candle in the West.

Seat yourself before the Altar and go into meditation. You are to remain there for the next three hours in absolute silence. During this time you will seek, through Vision, the Realms of the Goddess and the God, observing and taking heed of everything your five inner senses are aware of.

This procedure must not be overlooked and you must take the time to be informed of your duties upon your Path and be prepared to follow through. When the time has been spent then return to the familiar dimension of the physical world.

Take the prepared oil and make the sign of the Pentagram over it with your Athame. Rub your entire body with the oil and say:

'I, N . . ., am properly prepared to take the Rite of Initiation at the hands of the Gods. I have within my Soul no fear and am committed to that which I seek. I have two perfect words . . . "Love" and "Trust" . . . and with all things I will uphold my oath rightly!'

Light all candles except the white Altar candle. Then light the Incense.

Consecrate the salt as follows:

'Blessings upon this crystal of the Sea forced from the Womb of the Mother by the might of the Sacred Sun!'

Now make the sign of the Pentagram over it with your Athame. Consecrate the water by holding your Athame blade within it and saying:

'Out of thee, water creature, goes all that is not pure. May only the essence of the Great Mother remain!'

Place the wine into the Cup and place the blade of your Athame into it saying:

'The Cup is the symbol of Woman and the Goddess. The Athame is the symbol of Man and God; co-joined they are the Blessed Union that produces the Three Drops of Inspiration, the Creation Continuous!'

Now stand and take the Incense around the Circle holding

it up in silence at each of the Gateways starting at the East and ending there; place the thurible at the Eastern Gateway. Then take up the Pentacle and, starting at the Southern Gateway go around the Circle holding it up at each Gateway and ending at the South again, where you will place the Pentacle. Now take up the Water and, starting at the West repeat the above ending at the Western Gateway where you will leave the Cup. Take up the gold candle and go from North to North holding the candle aloft at each Gateway and leaving it at the Northern Gateway.

Return to the Altar and take the Salt and add it to the Water in the West. Kneel there and close off all orifices (for woman, 13; for man, 12.) with the salt and water saying:

'The protections of the Goddess be upon Her unborn Child!'

Return to the Altar and kneel.

Raise your Athame high and say:

'I, N . . ., in the presence of the Goddess and the God, give my solemn and sacred oath that I will abide by my Chosen Path and will seek to do the Will of the Gods without question. I shall keep silent all things entrusted to me by the Gods and by those who seek silence of me, in the true nature of the Priestess (Priest).

'I hereby take upon myself the life of a Witch and Priestess (Priest) and give my chosen Secret Name; N . . .! I am Thine!'

Now take the silver Pentagram from the Altar and go around the Circle and hold it up to each Gateway saying:

'See, O Ye Mighty Ones of the East! I hold before Thee the Symbol of my Priesthood with the Gods!'

Repeat for the South, West and North.

Go to the Western Gateway and dip the Amulet in the Salt and Water saying:

'I call the blessings of the Element of Water upon this Amulet! Acknowledge me, N . . ., Priestess (Priest) and Witch!'

Go to the North and hold the Amulet over the gold Candle saying:

'I call the blessings of the Element of Fire upon this Amulet! Acknowledge me, N ..., Priestess (Priest) and Witch!'

Go to the East and hold the Amulet over the Incense saying:

'I call the blessings of the Element of Air upon this Amulet! Acknowledge me, N ..., Priestess (Priest) and Witch!'

Go the South and place the Amulet upon the Pentacle saying:

'I call upon the Element of Earth to bless this Amulet of the Child of the Earth Mother! I am N ..., Priestess (Priest) and Witch!'

Return to the Altar and place the Amulet around your neck. Take up the Wine and form the sign of the Pentagram upon your forehead saying:

'Be it Sealed! I am Daughter of the Moon (Son of the Sun), Child of the First-born and Priestess (Priest) of my Rebirth, I shall never forsake the Seed of the Awakening and shall serve the Mighty Ones as has been done since the Island at the Dawn of all Knowledge!'

Now take up each of your Ritual tools and kiss them and say:

'Blessed Be!' to each one.

Then take up the Cup and raise it high and say:

'Now listen to the words of the Great Mother who was of old called Isis, Cerridwen, Hecate, Artemis, Astarte, Ishtar, Athena, Rhea, Diana, Melusine, Aphrodite, Dana, Bride and many other Names ...

Whenever ye have need of anything, Once in the Month and better it Be when the Moon is Full, then shall ye assemble in some Secret Place and Adore the Spirit of Me Who is Queen of All Witches. There shall ye assemble, ye who are fain to learn all Sorcery but have not yet learned its

Deeper Secrets. To these will I teach things that are yet
unknown. And ye shall be Free from Slavery and as a Sign
that ye be truly Free ye shall sing, dance, make music and
love all in My praise. For Mine is the Spirit of Ecstasy and
Mine, also is the joy on Earth; for My Law is Love Unto All
Things. Keep pure your Highest Ideals; let naught stop you
or turn you aside for Mine is the Secret Door of Youth and
Mine is the Cup of the Wine of Life and the Cauldron of
Immortality.

I am the Gracious Goddess Who gives the gift of joy unto
the heart of All. Upon Death I give Peace and Freedom and
True Knowledge of that which has gone before. Nor do I
demand sacrifice for behold! I am Mother of All Living and
My Love is poured forth upon the Earth!'

Then down the contents of the Cup and strike the Cup three
times with your Athame saying:

'So Mote It Be!'

Then seat yourself before the Altar and oil the white Candle
saying:

'In the Names of the Goddess and the God of my Chosen
Path I consecrate thee!'

The White Candle is to be kept in case you ever enact
Initiation upon another person where it is to be burned as the
Altar Candle.

Now stand and recast the Circle with your Athame speaking
your new Name to the East, South, West and North as you
go.

Seat yourself before the Altar and raise a soft humming
chant to centre yourself and relax in meditation for a while
before you close the Circle.

The Rite is done.

Before you go to sleep that night chant your Name
saying:

'I am N . . ., Priestess (Priest) and Witch!' until you fall
asleep.

Blessed Be!

Some Examples of a 'Working'

I am including here only those workings that I consider safe for a person who has not been trained through a suitable Coven; the reason being that you can get yourself into considerable hot water by attempting to alter the natural flow of your own circumstances, let alone anyone else's. Of course, I consider it natural that you will in some way attempt to do Spellcraft at some time so may I, therefore, offer some precautionary advice? You must take into account how far you can interfere without having the Spell rebound upon you; the Laws of 'cause and effect' ascertain that you will in some way *always* be affected by the work that you do, so keep it aligned to good intent or else be prepared for your world to topple about your ears. A few examples of Spells that usually go wrong:

— love spells

— money spells

— those relating to position

— retribution or revenge

— emotional, physical, spiritual or intellectual blackmail

The most acceptable 'change' Spells are those which are used when defence against unnecessary hardship will assist you with your Path. The thing to remember is that when you have taken upon yourself the Path as Witch you have placed yourself very definitely in the lap of the Gods, and they call the tune. They may force you into an impossible corner to get you to change the course of action that is not in alignment with Their calling of your Priesthood and you must seek guidance from Them and trust in the answers. Even though Their requirements of you may not fit into your planned future you will find, in retrospect, that the reasons are obvious. You may seek to understand what They wish through whatever means is available to you. I use Tarot or Inner Plane Accessibility to clarify the changes but any form of divination that is comfortable for you will achieve results: They will never leave you to flounder aimlessly in indecision and their answers are always accessible. Trust in your intuition at all times, as this is the voice of higher guidance.

It is also to be understood that if you have done the training herein your Spells will almost always work so take heed of the warnings.

Note: Never accept payment, even if offered!

The House Blessing
This procedure applies whether in your own or someone else's house.

You will need your Wand and a container of previously consecrated water and salt. Always protect yourself prior to the working by closing all your orifices with the salt and water and invoking the assistance of the Goddess and the Four Elements.

You are to use the salt and water liberally. Firstly go around the house from the outside and cast a permanent Circle of protection sprinkling the water and saying:

'May the Lady and Lord cause all malignity to be henceforth withheld from this place and may what transpires within be only that which is of the greatest good of all who dwell so protected!'

Then proceed to draw the sign of the Pentagram on every door and window of the place concentrating on banishing all past disturbances from either the people now occupying the dwelling or past tenants.

Go within and proceed from room to room. Raise your Wand from floor to ceiling in each corner of each room, creating a pillar of Fire (in its cleansing aspect) and join each pillar to form a circle boundary saying:

'I banish all malignity and hindrance from this place and

all that is no longer of this Plane but tarries must leave now of free will to pass to higher realms! This I proclaim in the Names of the Goddess and the God and in the balance of the Elements that represent Them! So Mote It Be!'

Go through this procedure in each room, remembering to sprinkle the consecrated water around you as you proceed. Inform the people dwelling there that unresolved anger and all such emotions will slowly erode the blessing and that the avoidance of such will enhance their lives both personally and environmentally.

On your way out stop at the front gate and draw the sign of the Pentagram upon the ground and say:

'Peace be the Name of this place! So Mote It Be!'

If it is your own home that you have blessed then return indoors and cast a Circle, and meditate your thanks to the Forces for their assistance; the same applies with the place of another person but always wait until you are in the sanctuary of your own home.

The Practising Witch

You will find Witches in almost every avenue of life. Most will not discuss their beliefs with you unless they are sure of who you are. Some have tried to dispel the ignorance and bigotry of centuries; some are blatant and obviously open to questioning; many are silent. All respect the rights of others to practise their religion peacefully but many are embittered at the arrogance of those who 'blindly' call us 'devil worshippers' (and just in case there are other than interested parties reading this let me inform you that to believe and hence worship this 'devil' one first needs to be a member of the Christian faith — Witches are not!). Who is to say, ultimately, who is right and who is fooling themselves? I have known, in this day and age, of a woman and her family who were literally burned from their home in the Western Suburbs of Sydney! Others, like me, have been harassed by local church bureaucrats who know absolutely nothing valid about our practices. I have a friend who is a well-respected American Witch who arrived at a New Moon gathering in a taxi; it is not always the practice in America to be coy about the Craft and so she came in the cab in robes, with her Athame in her belt and Wand in hand only to be asked by the driver if she was going to a fancy-dress party!

I once lectured a class of computer programming students — the teacher, a very enlightened woman, wished them to learn to think laterally — and I asked them 'Who here doesn't believe in Witches?' Most of them raised their hands. I then asked how many of them were Christians and most of them raised their hands, so I said 'Well, I don't believe in you!' That is also a peculiar phenomenon that has been invoked in the general public out of fear for the wart-nosed old hag with the hump-back and broomstick. (I only possess the third!)

Witches (some prefer the word 'Wiccans') can be found almost anywhere and are distinguished only by those who know what to look for — laughter and unashamed passion for living, anger at unjust laws against both humankind and Nature; they are, however, usually recognised by their own kind by either the Amulet they wear or by certain phrases that are meaningful only amongst ourselves.

Some have gone 'public' and have tried to eradicate the 'bad' image to little or no avail. But slowly, slowly do the Times change! Anti-discrimination Acts are our first call; the right to practise one's own religion without interference from others is a part of our democratic constitution.

Women are among the first to accept and acknowledge the Goddess, having long fought the oppression of patriarchal systems in all areas of life, especially religion. Within this liberation they have reached out and have been touched by the wings of the Lady. They feel within themselves the bonding of their own sex and the taste of the glory of freedom. Men who become Witches do so from their own callings and for their own reasons. Having discussed this matter with many male Witches, I find that they no longer accept their own limitations or those of a society that undermines compassion, nurturing, loving and regards them as the past-time of women (and therefore a sign of weakness!). Witchcraft has them wallowing in their own newly-formed liberation. That, surely, above many other reasons, is paramount — that we walk together in our strengths and do not allow separatism to be our undoing upon this planet!

Those Witches who work on the development of their psychic talents, or who are endowed with them already, quite often leave the mundane work-force and offer their gifts in such fields as divination, numerology, astrology etc., therefore becoming poor man's psychologists. Many are excellent at these practices and will aid those who cannot receive help from any other area. Some grow herbs, others are gifted in the healing arts, some make talismans, amulets, sometimes call the rain, ofttimes banish 'No Standing' signs and have no problem finding parking places and very, very rarely do we close our doors to anyone in need.

We have few Laws; whatever we do returns threefold. Our motto is, 'Do what ye Will so long as ye harm none, never boast never threaten'; and this covers just about everything, doesn't it? We never give the location of other Covensteads or the identity of other Witches unless they so request.

We have no functioning moral code as all loving is rightful in the eyes of the Lady and Lord so long as it harms not. We fight suffering, intolerance, greed, bigotry, animosity and destructive acts, as these things are anathema to our beliefs.

Whether a Witch works within a traditional Coven structure or alone as a Solitary matters not in the long run; a Priestess or Priest of the Ancient Seed is a Priestess or Priest twenty-four hours of the day; they work the Rites to the High Gods and by their right as Initiates work their Will upon the Earth in a religion of Balance to both the Forces of the Elementals upon this planet and the Forces of Universal Source known to us as the Spiral Dance!

Walk in Peace upon the Earth Mother's Breast.

Table of Correspondences 1: The Elements

Element:	Tarot:	Zodiacal:	Planetary:	Colour:	Plant:	Other:
Fire:	Wands	Aries (1) Leo (5) Sagittarius (9)	Mars Sun Jupiter	Red (and all associated colours).	Nettle	North (Southern Hemisphere)* midday Summer
Water:	Cups	Cancer (4) Scorpio (8) Pisces (12)	Moon Pluto Neptune	Green (and all associated colours)	Lotus (and all water plants)	West (Southern Hemisphere) sunset Spring
Earth:	Pentacles	Taurus (2) Virgo (6) Capricorn (10)	Venus Mercury Saturn	Yellow (and all associated colours)	Red Poppy	South (Southern Hemisphere)* midnt. Winter
Air:	Swords	Gemini (3) Libra (7) Aquarius (11)	Mercury Venus Uranus	Blue (and all associated colours)	Aspen, Mistletoe	East (Southern Hemisphere) sunrise Autumn

* Positions of North and South reversed in Northern Hemisphere.

Table of Correspondences 2: Planetary Symbols

Planet:	Colour:	Plant:	Metal:	Gem:	Perfume:	Day:	Animal:
Sun:	Yellow, Gold	Sunflower Heliotrope	Gold	Topaz Yellow diamond	Olibanum Wood-aloes	Sunday	Lion Phoenix
Moon:	Violet, Silver	Hazel, Almond	Silver	Quartz Crys. Moonstone	Camphor Jasmine Rose	Monday	Elephant
Mercury:	Orange	Vervain, Cinquefoil	Quicksilver	Agate Amber	Narcissus Storax	Wednesday	Jackal Twin-serpents
Venus:	Green	Myrtle, Fennel, Vervain	Copper	Emerald Jade	Amber-gris Benzoin	Friday	Lynx
Mars:	Scarlet	Absynth Rue	Iron	Ruby	Sulphur Tobacco	Tuesday	Basilisk

	Color	Plant	Metal	Stone	Incense	Day	Animal
Jupiter:	Blue	Oak, Agrimony, Olive	Tin	Sapphire Lapis	Aloes Oakmoss Balm	Thursday	Centaur Unicorn
Saturn:	Indigo, Black	Ash, Rowan, Cyprus	Lead	Onyx Jet Obsidian	Myrrh Alum Nightqueen	Saturday	Woman
Uranus:	White	Amaranth	Uranium	Turquoise	Musk Hemp		Man
Neptune:	Green/ black	Seaweed	Borax	Coral			Dolphin
Pluto:	Blue/ black	Roots of most plants, Mandrake	Plutonium	Bloodstone	Opium Asafoetida		Scorpion

Suggested Reading

Witchcraft
Starhawk, *The Spiral Dance*, Harper & Row, San Francisco
   1979
Starhawk, *Dreaming the Dark*, Beacon Press, Boston 1982
Stewart Farrar, *What Witches Do*, Phoenix Books, Washington
   1983
Janet & Stewart Farrar, *The Witches' Way*, Hale, London
   1984
Janet & Stewart Farrar, *Eight Sabbats for Witches*, Hale, London
   1981
Justine Glass, *Witchcraft, the Sixth Sense and Us*, Spearman,
   London 1965
Doreen Valiente, *An ABC of Witchcraft Past and Present*, Robert
   Hale Ltd, London
Doreen Valiente, *Witchcraft for Tomorrow*, Robert Hale Ltd,
   London

Qabalah (Kabbalah)
Alan Richardson, *Introduction to the Mystical Qabalah*, Thorsons,
   Northamptonshire 1982
Alan Richardson, *The Gate of Moon*, Thorsons, Northampton-
   shire 1984
Israel Regardie, *A Garden of Pomegranates*, Llewellyn, Minnesota
   1970
Dion Fortune, *The Mystical Qabalah*, Benn, London 1965
Aryeh Kaplan, *Meditation and Kabbalah*, Weiser, Maine 1983

Magic

Aleister Crowley, *Magick*, Routledge & Kegan Paul, London 1973

Nevill Drury, *Don Juan, Mescalito and Modern Magic*, Routledge & Kegan Paul, London 1978

Nevill Drury, *The Occult Experience*, Hale, London 1987

Myth

J.G. Frazer, *The Golden Bough*, Macmillan, London 1963

Mircea Eliade, *Patterns in Comparative Religion*, Sheed & Ward, London 1958

Definite Ex Libris . . .

Barbara G. Walker, *Encyclopedia of Women's Mysteries*, Harper & Row, San Francisco 1983

Dolores Ashcroft-Nowicki, *The Shining Paths*, Aquarian Press, Northamptonshire 1983

Dolores Ashcroft-Nowicki, *First Steps in Ritual*, Aquarian Press, Northamptonshire 1982

Nor Hall, *The Moon and the Virgin*, Harper & Row, New York 1980.

NOTES

NOTES

NOTES

NOTES

NOTES

NOTES

NOTES

NOTES

NOTES

NOTES

NOTES

NOTES